W9-BRF-398

INNOVATION, INC.

Unlocking Creativity in the Workplace

**Stephen R. Grossman, Bruce E. Rodgers
and
Beverly R. Moore**

**Illustrated by
Richard D. Pinney**

Wordware Publishing, Inc.

Library of Congress Cataloging-in-Publication Data

Grossman, Stephen R.
  Innovation Inc. : unlocking creativity in the.
  work-place.

  Includes index.
  1. Creative ability in business.   I. Rodgers,
  Bruce E.   II. Moore, Beverly R.   III. Title.
  HD53.G76   1988   658.3'14   88-10616
  ISBN 1-55622-054-5

© 1988 Wordware Publishing, Inc.

All Rights Reserved

1506 Capital Ave.
Plano, Texas 75074

No part of this book may be reproduced in any form or by any means
without permission in writing from Wordware Publishing, Inc.

Printed in the United States of America

ISBN 1-55622-054-5

10 9 8 7 6 5 4 3 2 1
8803

All inquiries for volume purchases of this book should be
addressed to Wordware Publishing, Inc., at the above address.
Telephone inquiries may be made by calling:

(214) 423-0090

About the Authors

Stephen R. Grossman

Stephen R. Grossman, President of Double Dominance Inc., of Maple Shade, NJ, has taught, trained, and consulted in creativity, problem solving, and corporate innovation for the past decade. His fifteen years of industrial experience as a physical scientist included the directorship of a basic research team in new product development for a Fortune 500 company.

Aside from a number of technical awards, Grossman is the holder of several patents for new consumer products and manufacturing technologies, including the one for Cottonelle® bathroom tissue. He is also the author of many papers on the relationship between creativity and technical problem solving, and has served as vice chairman of the International Paper Physics Committee of the Technical Association of the Pulp and Paper Industry.

Grossman is on the faculty of the Creative Institute in Buffalo, and is also a member of American Mensa. He has appeared on many television and radio shows to discuss the relationship of creativity to problem solving and organizational innovation.

Bruce E. Rodgers

Bruce E. Rodgers brings a lifetime of creative activity to his work as a consultant and trainer in problem solving and corporate innovation — most recently in the design and development of micro-computer software and as a technical writer. As a guest lecturer, workshop leader, and teacher, he has addressed community groups and organizations in the field of creativity throughout the Northeast.

Mr. Rodgers personally applies his creative philosophies as an accomplished playwright, and he is resident playwright at Princeton's McCarter Theatre, a major American not-for-profit regional theatre. He has won playwriting grants from the New Jersey State Council on the Arts, and has had his work performed by the McCarter Theatre, as well as the GeVa Theatre in Rochester, NY. In addition, he consults for the New Jersey State Council on the Arts as a playwriting panel member, as a professional theatre on-site evaluator, and as a creative liaison and facilitator.

Beverly R. Moore

Beverly R. Moore, President of CHOICE POINT ASSOCIATES, is a Human Resource Development and Marketing Specialist. She received her Bachelor of Arts degree from Augustana College, Rock Island Illinois, and has done advanced study at Harvard University, Cambridge, Massachusetts, and State University College of New York, Buffalo, New York. In addition, Ms. Moore has trained with University Associates, San Diego, California, and Synectics Inc., Cambridge, Massachusetts.

Ms. Moore established CHOICE POINT, a meeting-training center in Duxbury, Massachusetts, in 1979. She heads a corps of skilled, multi-disciplinary consultants.

With over twelve years of experience, Beverly Moore has designed and conducted training for more than 4,000 people in over 500 business, industrial, govermental, educational, and community organizations. She has been an instructor for Boston University, State University College of New York, Rensselaer Polytechnic Institute, and Bridgewater State College. For over three years, Ms. Moore has been researching and developing applications of brain dominance technology in areas of management and marketing. She is certified and has administered over 400 Herrmann Brain Dominance Surveys for corporate and individual analysis.

Because of Beverly Moore's excellent reputation in producing tangible results through practicing what she teaches, the volunteer sector has called upon her to serve in many leadership and management roles. She has chaired many boards of directors, finance committees, major fund-raising campaigns and has served as a consultant to the National Center for Voluntary Action in Washington, D.C.

Acknowledgements

If I have seen further, it is by standing on the shoulders of giants.
— Isaac Newton

Every creative act is a manipulative exercise. We take what exists, reshape and reconnect it in some different context to solve a problem. The same is true for this book. Many of the ideas and concepts are direct outgrowths of several outstanding contributors to the field of creative studies.

The use of analogies for problem solving and the concept of dissecting ideas were originally developed by George Prince and Bill Gordon in their Synectics model. Brainstorming was first suggested by Walt Disney in the late 1920s, and expanded and updated by Alex Osborn in the late 1950s.

Doctor Edward deBono's treatises on lateral thinking provided material for becoming the "Angel's Advocate." Also, Ned Herrmann's work on Brain Dominance provides much of the insight about the Four Faces of Creativity. Credit is also due to Dr. Robert Weisberg, Professor of Psychology at Temple University, whose research suggested the framework on which some of our models are based.

Credit for some of the anecdotes and the general creative problem solving methodology go to Sidney Parnes, Ruth Noller, and Angelo Biondi of the Creative Problem Solving Institute (CPSI) in Buffalo, NY. We must also thank our CPSI presenting colleagues for their continuing fellowship and inspiration in the field of creative thinking.

Thanks to Ed Wiseman of B.F. Goodrich for sharing his expertise in corporate creative problem solving, and to Eugene Raudsepp for his help developing the Choice Point Brain Dominance Survey.

We owe Ed Carrington, Joe Weinkam, Roy Bostic, and Linda Kinsey our gratitude for reading the manuscript and sharing their honest, constructive comments.

Thanks are also due to Katherine Catlin, who unselfishly gave her ideas, suggestions, and encouraging words to help make the book what it has become.

We owe a special debt to our clients who have validated the effectiveness of creative problem solving by using the skills incorporated in this book to produce creative results.

Finally, special thanks to our friends and relatives who provided the inspiration and support for us to complete this project.

Contents

Chapter 1

The Competitive Edge

*Eight Fundamental
Principles of Creativity*

Regardless of what you do for a living, increasing your ability to think creatively will do more to move you toward personal and professional success than anything else you could do.

Creative thinking involves the ability to find solutions to problems by changing your point of view when normal channels fail to give you the answers you need. The more innovative the solutions are to your business and career challenges, the more competitive you will be in the market. Easy answers are for everyone. Creative answers are for the best.

Innovation, Inc. describes our way of stimulating creative thinking, selling new ideas once they are developed, and implementing them once they are sold. Developed over fifteen years, the process has been successfully used with governmental agencies such as NASA, and with large corporations such as IBM, AT&T, Johnson & Johnson, Scott Paper Co., and many others. However, it has been equally successful in a multitude of small and middle-sized businesses and not-for-profit organizations. Marketing, finance, human resources, research and development, management information services (MIS), manufacturing — virtually all management areas have used this collection of skills, methods, techniques, and exercises to turn their most difficult problems into implementable, profitable opportunities.

If you use this book, either by working all the exercises or simply reading through for the concepts, and if you commit to incorporating the techniques into your daily routine, you will soon find yourself:

1. Discovering opportunities and solving problems with increasingly innovative insights.
2. Selling your new and creative ideas with increasing effectiveness.
3. Implementing the ideas you have just developed and sold.

As you read these pages, you will find proven systems for accomplishing each of these. And when these three steps actually happen, you and your business will reap the rewards of being first, of being distinctive, of being the best. This is the promise of this book.

To take full advantage of INNOVATION, INC., it is important to understand eight fundamental principles and assumptions upon which it rests:

1. Everyone is creative.
2. Creativity reduces risk.
3. There are four faces of creativity.
4. One does not live by data alone.
5. One picture is worth *more* than a thousand words.
6. There are no impossible dreams or problems (only limited dreamers and problem solvers).
7. The subconscious is a full partner in the creative process.
8. Creative thinking creates win/win situations (without compromise).

As we explore each of these principles, ask yourself how it relates to you, to your work, and to your business.

EVERYONE IS CREATIVE

Many people feel that because they have never played a musical instrument or were unable to draw well or never invented anything, they are not creative and they have resigned themselves to a non-creative life. We find people in this situation time and again in our consulting. If you have spent your adult life telling yourself you are not creative, you are wrong: you are simply out of practice.

Think about it. Have you ever taken a new route home from work because of a problem with the old one? Have you ever changed the way you communicated with a problem employee because you were not getting through? Have you ordered a different dish in your favorite restaurant because you were tired of the same old fare? If you have done any of the above, you have been creative. That really is all it takes.

The fact is, creativity is intrinsic to your life. As a human being, it is something you are, regardless of where and how it is exercised. It stems from the fact that we are all unique creations. We are *all* individuals. While the composer is limited to twelve notes on the scale, and the painter to using the colors red, yellow, and blue, the primary colors from which all the other hues are derived; you are the quintessential creation, with elements to arrange and combine which nobody but you possesses.

When you look at it from that point of view, being creative should not be all that difficult. For if each of us can figure out how to express in our work that wonderful uniqueness which is our *self*, we should all find ourselves creative masters — and very successful.

Actually, you are probably ten times more creative than you realize. You are engaged in productive work. Products are being conceived, designed, produced, shipped and sold. You put out ten fires a week, duck three political bullets a month, meet impossible quotas every quarter, and somehow pull off an annual miracle. Problems of all sizes get solved, the work gets done, and business goes on. Numbers and reports and computers are not doing this work. You are. And you are doing it by creating, by developing ideas which solve problems and meet challenges.

That does not mean, however, that you can not be more creative than you already are. You can be better than you are. You *can* improve the quality and originality of your ideas. We know this is possible because, as consultants, it has become our way of life, as well as that of the clients we guide. Over the years, we have led thousands of people to fresh, innovative concepts through the creative techniques in this book. We have seen them change the way they approach problems, the way they interact with ideas, and the way they prepare themselves to receive the answers they need.

Accomplishing the change is a matter of believing the change *can* happen, learning and mastering the necessary skills, and incorporating them into your daily attitudes and actions.

We will share the skills with you, suggest ways to help you master them, and assist you in finding ways to incorporate them into your life. By consciously using and developing your innate creative ability, you will become an *actively* creative person. The commitment and the belief begins now. It may not seem easy, and it will cost you some time, but the return quickly outweighs the investment.

CREATIVITY REDUCES RISK

the ability to take anything and make something from it

Actively creative people are often considered risk-takers. Surprisingly, though, it is our experience that the opposite is true. People living creative lives take far *fewer* risks than those who believe themselves uncreative.

This is so because creative people are secure in their ability to take any outcome and make something from it. They are "opportunity thinkers." To them, problems, glitches, and failures represent challenges, not obstacles. Where some people might accept failure as an ending, creative people see it as another branch in an evolutionary process where success is the inevitable result.

History is full of examples of inventions, innovations and profitable products which sprang from failed attempts at developing something completely different. Products like 3M's Post-its,™ Proctor and Gamble's Ivory Soap, vulcanized rubber products, Silly Putty, and the successful weed-killer 2,4-D were all developed or improved by accident or mistake. They were failures. Flops. But a person with a vigorous creative pulse took that flop and flipped it into something profitable.

Actively creative people develop a heightened ability for "seeing" potential in *any* situation. They develop an immunity to the fear of failure since failure is never an ending, it is the departure point for the next creative challenge. Ideas and notions which seem to be failures are constantly turned around, flipped upside down and inside out to see what can be made from them.

By allowing yourself to live up to your creative potential, you are actually protecting yourself *against* failure and, therefore, eliminating risk. Creative thinking is the ultimate insurance.

THERE ARE FOUR FACES OF CREATIVITY

In our consulting work, we have found four different types of people. Perhaps you have seen them around, too. The first type might work in finance; we will call him Walt. If Walt is not in audit, he should be, since he displays a dazzling agility with figures. He reads balance sheets as a hobby, and he smells funny numbers three pages away. If you want to sell him, you better flood your presentation with data, because his thirst for facts is insatiable. And you do not offer Walt wine at a company party without knowing its vintage.

The second type we see holds a position such as Director of Personnel. Kathleen, we will call her, is one of the best organized people you have ever met. She carries off an impossibly busy schedule with aplomb, gliding effortlessly from appointment to appointment on a steady stream of neatly printed lists. And you should see Kathleen throw a dinner party. Each course magically appears at the table on time and piping hot, and the seating plan bears striking resemblance to the organization chart. A glance at her bookshelf reveals a first edition copy of *The One Minute Manager* and a record collection in alphabetical order.

Sandy holds a job such as marketing manager for one of the small, entrepreneurial business units. She is one of those people who is impossible to contact because no one knows where she is. In a meeting, you can plan on her being late, but you can also count on her having ten ideas to everyone else's two. Since she is rarely doing less than two things simultaneously, do not be upset if she is writing her management report during your dry-run sales presentation. But when you are through she will be the only one who understood the overall concept. If you root around her chaotic office, you will find a sign which says: "If you think my desk is cluttered, you should see my mind."

You might find the fourth type out in field sales. Everyone loves Bob. He is the kind of person you would trust with your most intimate secrets because you know he would never do anything to hurt your feelings. He is a good listener and a good laugher, and people instantly feel comfortable talking to him. However, do not bother asking him if he is free to work late. He belongs to four clubs and coaches in three leagues.

Do you recognize Walt, Kathleen, Sandy, and Bob? Do you have people like them in your group or business? They may also resemble customers or vendors. Who are you most like?

Even though many people tend to resemble one general style, we actually have some of all four living within us. We all have a little bit of Walter the analyzer, Kathleen the implementor, Sandy the "imaginator" (our word for someone with a strong preference for imaginative thinking), and Bob the collaborator. Together, they comprise the four faces of creativity, the four fundamental thinking styles. And all four styles are necessary for true, useful innovation.

For example, last year Walt perceived a need for a more accurate inventory tracking system in his business, and the imaginator in him dreamed up a totally fresh approach to the process. The collaborator in him helped him understand the needs of the inventory department by talking with each of the people who would use the system. Then his analyzer figured out the procedural logic. And finally, his implementor managed the project, overseeing the timely training, installation, and activation of the system.

Often, the imaginator style is the only style perceived as being "creative," thus many logical, procedural people consider themselves uncreative. They may have "artistic" friends they consider creative, and they see little similarity between those friends and themselves.

However, *all* styles are creative, with each expressing their creativity differently. Walt creates his unique inventory system, while Kathleen reorganizes a division. Sandy dreams up a brilliant, off-the-wall marketing plan, while Bob figures out how to snatch the competition's largest account.

Ideas alone are not enough to be innovative. Useful ideas must be separated from the impractical, they must be implemented with a measure of discipline and technique, in a way that others can understand and use them.

Think about your own work. What parts of your responsibilities are analytical? What parts require organizational skills? Imaginative skills? Collaborative skills? Try drawing four columns and looking at your job from these four points of view.

The key is to recognize the Walt, Kathleen, Sandy, and Bob within yourself, and within your organization, and then manage and develop them for their strengths. *Each* one of them contributes to the process of innovation. It is a team effort. And you are that team of four.

ONE DOES NOT LIVE BY DATA ALONE

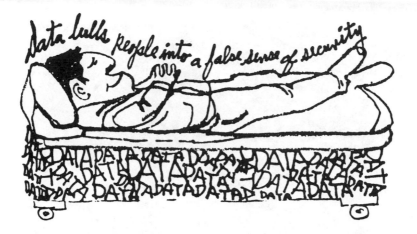

There is little information you have that your competitor doesn't have, and if he doesn't have it, he can get it, or he's in the process of getting it. What you *do* with your information, what you see in it, what you can make from it, how creative you are with it is what makes the difference.

They say you can not be too rich, too thin, too good looking, or have too much data. No doubt, we live and work in a data-oriented society. And the computer revolution has put more information, and the analytical tools to manipulate it, at the fingertips of more people than ever before. We can literally bury ourselves in information just by turning on a printer and letting it run.

However, data is only the raw material for solutions, just as paint is the raw material for art. Paint does not become art until the artist creates something with it. Data alone does not design, build, or sell products. Data does not make employees want to be more productive, and it does not make them care about the quality of their work. Data alone has nothing to do with the bottom line, with the profitability of your business. Only people have that kind of impact.

It is people who take information and turn it into a new product, or a better product, or a more distinctive product. It is people who take data on quality control and turn it into a new way to make hourlies on the assembly line care about the return rate on their product. It is the merchant who uses her mailing list in a new and unusual way to make a significant increase in sales.

An emphasis on data lulls people into a false sense of security. Because facts are so concrete, so defendable, it is too often a comfortable place to stop in the search for solutions. Unfortunately, solutions based solely on data are hollow, and far weaker than they appear. The subjective input of the human mind *using* qualified data as fuel for imaginative leaps is vital for solid, trustworthy answers.

ONE PICTURE IS WORTH MORE THAN A THOUSAND WORDS

O, my Luve is like a red, red rose,
That's newly sprung in June.
— Robert Burns

Even if your product [quality] gets better right away, it takes time for
the public to realize it. It is like the bad girl in town who changes her
ways and goes straight. For the first couple of years, nobody believes her.
— Lee Iacocca

The image, the metaphor, the analogy, the simile, the symbol — these are all at the very heart of the creative process. They are expressions or pictures which compare or represent the qualities of two seemingly dissimilar things. In the quotations above, Robert Burns finds that his "Luve" and a red rose share common qualities, while Lee Iacocca likens a change in product quality to the reform of the town vamp. Both the poem's image and Iacocca's analogy create pictures which convey much, much more than the literal meaning of the words.

But images and analogies are also the conduit for innovative ideas. For example, early in the space program, when astronauts in bulky space suits could not join items together with existing fasteners, designers found a solution by looking for an analogy in the world of nature for things which "attach." This thinking led them to the cocklebur which clings so well to your slacks when you walk through a field, and hence the birth of Velcro.

When one of our clients, lacking a coordinating manager between marketing and manufacturing, was searching for ways to foster spontaneous cooperation between the two groups, they found an analogy in the world of music: the jam session, from which they discovered many potential solutions.

Images, analogies, metaphors, etc. give you the whole picture at once, in a single, succinct, powerful package. They allow you to deal with a creative challenge in a completely different context, away from the knotty specifics of the problem itself, in a different "world" where a similar problem has already been solved. The jam session, with its smoke-filled rooms and individual contributors spontaneously and harmoniously working in a group context, is a perfect example.

It is no coincidence that the words "image" and "imagination" have the same root. One (image) fuels the other (imagination). Einstein came to his theory of relativity by imagining he was riding through space on a beam of light. *The image took him to the insight.*

You use and experience image, metaphor, and simile constantly. They paint your conversation ("They're selling like hot cakes.") and bombard you in advertising ("Reach out and touch someone.") Think, for a minute, about the expressions you use, how often do you incorporate simile when you speak? Does your business have an "image?" If you have a logo, what kinds of ideas and feelings are communicated by it? Look at your letterhead, what does the typeface communicate? If your business was a vehicle, what would it be? A Rolls? A pickup? A Corvette? Why?

Consciously applied as an agent for innovation, thinking in images and analogies is like reading a treasure map. It shows you the route, the milestones, and pinpoints the treasure. All that is left is for you to follow it, and dig.

THERE ARE NO IMPOSSIBLE DREAMS OR PROBLEMS
(Only Limited Dreamers and Problem Solvers)

> "It can not be done. We've tried everything, and it just can't be done."

Look at that sentence. Presented out of context, it sounds a little ridiculous, does it not? Yet in context with the seemingly impossible problems of your business (or your life) it is probably something you have said or felt more than once. The fact is, other than *giving* your product or service away, there is nothing as damaging to your long-term success and profitability as the sincere acceptance of that statement. Nothing.

The reason it is so damaging is that it is false. There are solutions for whatever problem you are experiencing. Not a solution, but solutions — more than one. When we say this to people, seven out of ten reply, "Sure, but you don't understand our situation." It doesn't matter. We do not need to know the details of a particular problem to know it can be solved. We know there are solutions because throughout the history of man, there have *always* been solutions to insolvable problems. All it took was someone to recognize the answer.

We all know the list of significant discoveries and innovations: gun powder, fertilizer, bacteria, penicillin, vaccines, electricity, organized labor, radiation, public education, the internal combustion engine, flight, the computer, and these are only a few of the most significant. But there is a far longer list of day-to-day problems and situations which seemed every bit as impossible, and which found equally viable solutions. Sometimes those answers came immediately; other times it took centuries. But the answer has been there, always, waiting for someone to find it.

When you truly believe there is no answer to your problem, you are simply handing the advantage over to your competition. If you do not believe there is a way to produce your product twice as efficiently, and your competition does, he or she stands an infinitely better chance of finding it and beating you in the market. If you don't know in your heart that you can be doing what you do better, faster, or cheaper than you are now doing it, watch out. Someone else who is more creative than you are does believe it. And when they find it, you will discover yourself in second place and fading.

The most creative people *know* there are answers to every challenge. They instinctively understand that they must see the problem from a different point of view, and they commit their whole selves to this task. Those who do less, settle for less.

THE SUBCONSCIOUS IS A FULL PARTNER IN THE CREATIVE PROCESS

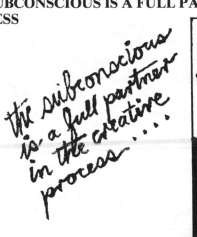

To generate ideas for meeting creative challenges, it is vital to trust the role of the subconscious. You will be the most creative by surrendering your challenge to it, believing it will give you the solution you need. If you make that commitment wholeheartedly, your subconscious mind will not let you down.

The subconscious is like a good office staff. It works on what it intuitively knows is important to you and needs no direction. It simply understands what you need and works tirelessly, without complaining, until the work is done.

Have you ever tried to remember someone's name, had it right on the tip of your tongue, but could not get it out to save your life? You might remember the face, every detail of what he or she wore the last time you were together, and even half the conversation. But for some reason, the name isn't there. After working at it for a few minutes, you get frustrated, give up, and forget about it.

Then, an hour later, eating lunch or driving to a sales call, the name leaps into your mind. You feel wonderful, as if you have just accomplished something difficult.

While you thought you had forgotten about it, you hadn't really. You had only *consciously* stopped thinking about it. All the while, your subconscious was working away. When the work was done and your conscious was finally relaxed enough, over lunch or in the car, not occupied with other important tasks, the answer rose to the surface, and you felt redeemed.

When you find yourself saddled with a different problem or in search of a truly innovative answer, and you cannot come up with it, it is often best to stop working on it for the present. Know that while you are doing other things, your subconscious continues to work. The answer might arrive in a dream, during the semi-conscious moments between sleep and waking, in the shower, or whenever the mind is relaxed and not intensely involved. Often people keep a pad and pencil by their bed just to record ideas before they are forgotten.

If you discount the subconscious and its role in the creative process, if you try to muscle your way to answers by only using your conscious mind, you are fighting with one arm behind your back. Let go. Relax. Have faith in your subconscious and it will reward you, time after time, with appropriate, innovative, implementable answers to the most complex challenges you face.

CREATIVE THINKING CREATES WIN/WIN SITUATIONS
(Without Compromise)

Have your cake and eat it, too. They say it cannot be done, but they are wrong: they are just not being creative. *Whenever* you find yourself in an either/or situation, it is nothing more than an invitation to creativity.

How many times have you been between two less-than-desirable options but felt forced to choose one or the other (political elections excluded)? How often have you been at loggerheads with a colleague over a particular business strategy, each of you pressing your own point of view? When have you felt like the immovable object to someone's irresistible force?

If you are in an American business, this scenario must be familiar to you because it is a national infection. Many companies actively or unconsciously promote win/lose as a management philosophy. "A little competition is healthy," they say. They encourage internal competition to develop the best ideas. Those whose ideas are accepted are winners, while those whose ideas are rejected are losers. Winners gain favor, promotion, bonuses; while losers — lose. This is what we mean by win/lose. Someone wins, someone loses.

Businesses which cultivate this environment are wrong. Competition is healthy *among* businesses, not *within* them. Internal competition encourages groups to hoard information and discourages the free flow of thinking and, thereby, restricts the cross fertilization of ideas. An internally competitive environment breaks down team-oriented behavior by creating internal we/they relationships.

A truly creative operating group establishes an environment where there are no winners and losers. When the group works on a problem, new solutions are found which incorporate the best elements of all ideas. Everyone contributes to the solution. Everyone wins. These are win/win situations.

There is no excuse for win/lose inside business. In fact, win/lose is simply evidence of an uncreative environment. When you find yourself painted into the win/lose corner, there is a hidden door, a secret passage for escape. And with a little searching, you will find it.

The creative solution accounts for the essential needs of all viewpoints without anyone having to compromise. It takes wasteful and frustrating opposing energies, and redirects them toward a new, previously unconsidered goal, satisfying the needs of all parties. Creative thinking changes conflict into confluence.

Unfortunately, finding the creative solution takes patience and considerable work. Somebody involved in the struggle must apply enough creative muscle to find a new solution in the first place. Then the other parties must be open enough to evaluate the idea fairly. When this occurs, the solution invigorates the atmosphere with the warmth of knowing that everyone has received what he needs without compromising anything. Everyone has won and everyone has been creative.

SUMMING UP

Look once again at the eight principles.

1. Everyone is creative.
2. Creativity reduces risk.
3. There are four faces of creativity.
4. One does not live by data alone.
5. One picture is worth *more* than a thousand words.
6. There are no impossible dreams or problems (only limited dreamers and problem solvers).
7. The subconscious is a full partner in the creative process.
8. Creative thinking creates win/win situations (without compromise).

As you continue with the book, and as you carry on your daily work, think about these principles as they apply to your creative opportunities and challenges. What principles do you see in yourself? In the people with whom you work? Which principles do you question?

A THOUGHT AND A CHALLENGE

Be emotionally involved! Most actively creative people are passionate about what they do, and this passion feeds both their intensity and their commitment. Intensity and commitment are essential ingredients of creative thought, bringing together *all* your resources, intellectual and emotional. As Rollo May states in *The Courage To Create*:

> We cannot *will* to have insights. We cannot *will* to have creativity. But we can *will* to give ourselves to the encounter [the creative experience] with intensity of dedication and commitment. The deeper aspects of the encounter are activated to the extent that the person is committed to the encounter.

To be creative, you *must* care. And the deeper your caring about the resolution, the more it means to you, the greater the resources you will bring to bear on the problem.

Now, to the challenge. We see this book as one in which you are an active contributor. Only you can take the steps to make it directly applicable to you and your business. With a piece of paper and a pen or pencil, write the following challenge:

How to get the maximum benefit from this book?

Throughout the remainder of the book, we will ask you to use our creative techniques to find insight into this challenge. We suggest you fold the paper into an appropriate size to use as a book mark, for its purpose is to help you keep your place in more than the obvious way.

The Basic Skills

*Four Necessary Skills
for Creative Thinking*

Face it, not only are your competitors out there dreaming up ideas for stealing your business, now even your non-competitors may enter your market next year, or next quarter, and they will be figuring out how to get their share, too. *Everyone* is hunting ideas for decreasing costs of materials, increasing product quality, decreasing labor costs, increasing worker productivity, decreasing overhead, increasing profit, etc. The companies which develop *and implement* the best ideas thrive. The rest are not long for this world.

The difference between the best companies and all the rest is how creatively they solve problems. The best companies think more, learn more, and create more than their competition. The creative process happens first. Then once they have discovered a solution, they implement it, and implement it more efficiently and effectively than anyone else.

FOUR SKILLS

This chapter discusses four skills essential for improving the way you find creative solutions to difficult problems. These skills are *necessary* if you are to be at your most innovative, for they, and their attendant techniques, when combined and integrated into your everyday thinking, are keys which open the doors to a truly creative life. They are the primary tools for constructing solutions to a wide range of personal and professional problems. The four essential skills are:

1. Divergent Thinking
2. Making Forced Relationships
3. Becoming the Angel's Advocate
4. Dissecting Ideas

Everything creative is a product of one or more of these skills consciously or subconsciously applied. They are what creative people *do*, and the better you are at them, the more innovative you will be.

The following example is a popular story in the creative field and one which aptly illustrates the creative process.

A group of management people in a small, mid-western corporation were having their weekly discussion of production problems and what to do about them. One of the issues involved a production loss because of the behavior and apparent lack of motivation of one the groups, the packers.

This group was responsible for wrapping the product in newspaper and then packing it in boxes for shipping. The problem was that the people spent more time reading the newspapers than packing the product. And needless to say, the packer's efficiency was less than sterling, however up-to-date they were.

After the usual idea of motivational talks was exhausted, someone suggested using blank paper to wrap the product. The management group was interested but discarded the notion because blank paper was too expensive. Someone else suggested "foreign language" newspapers. That idea wasn't bad, but it also failed because such papers were difficult to come by at this location.

Finally, in a moment of paramount frustration, common in management sessions like these, Pamela blurted out, "Why don't we just poke their eyes out?"

No sooner had the "idea" been uttered than Frank said in his calm and quiet way, "Hire blind people for the job."

This was it! Of course! What a great idea! And the group spent the rest of the meeting discussing the "blind people" notion.

Such issues as "What do we do with the people who are already on the line — we don't want unions coming in here?" were raised and needed resolution. But finally, it was decided that the blind would be integrated into the operation gradually, through attrition, and that the sighted people would be offered other positions where they would find new challenges and develop new skills without reading the news on company time.

In the end, the idea was a resounding success. Not only did the packer's efficiency show significant improvement, but the company rose to an important civic responsibility at the same time.

The critical turning point in that meeting was in the moment between the most ridiculous idea, "poke their eyes out," and the most significant one, "hire blind people." Look at each of the four essential skills in detail.

SKILL ONE — DIVERGENT THINKING

The thinking process has a split personality. We do two very different types of thinking, and each type has a distinctive personality. The first personality we call "the Judge," and the second we call "the Kid." The Judge and the Kid manage information in radically different ways.

The Kid   the judge

The Judge applies to that part of our thinking that evaluates. Looking at ideas or information, it makes one basic decision: acceptance or rejection. As far as the Judge is concerned, the decision is either thumbs up or thumbs down. Issues are black and white, with no gray area between.

The Judge draws conclusions by asking the following types of questions:

"Does it make sense?"
"Is it a good idea?"
"Is it logical?"

It is as if the Judge has a "window of acceptance," the shape of which is determined by prior experiences, prejudices, and knowledge. If the idea fits the shape of the space, it is accepted; if it doesn't, it is rejected. Decisions are made as a function of the fit.

We all do this so well that the Judge operates almost continually during our conscious hours at an automatic and subconscious level. And thank God! We make *so* many decisions minute by minute, that if we had to think much about them, we would never accomplish anything. The Judge takes care of that, and it is just as well.

The only problem comes when a simple yes/no, accept/reject, thumbs up/thumbs down doesn't supply us with a satisfactory solution. The Judge cannot deal with shades of gray, and when presented with something which cool logic fails to solve, it produces an automatic "no."

Fortunately for us, we have the Kid to bail us out. Characterized by a state of whimsy or arbitrariness, the Kid is also judgmental, but he comes to his judgment by asking questions very different from the Judge's.

Instead of questions which are easily answered with a yes or no, the Kid asks:

"Wow! Where can I go with this?"
"This is awesome, what can I do with it?"
"If this were true, then what would happen?"
"Why do I like this idea?"
"Why not?"

Because these questions allow for more open ended responses, we call this type of thinking *divergent thinking*. This thinking process allows your thoughts to diverge from the narrower confines of the problem, to wander into other related areas.

Convergent thinking narrows thought...

The Judge's thinking, on the other hand, asking for simple yes/no decisions, is termed *convergent thinking*. Convergent thinking narrows and focuses thoughts, reducing them to the point where logic may prevail.

The problem most of us have is that although the Kid exists in all of us, it is usually overshadowed by the size and significance of the Judge. It is only when we can somehow lock the Judge up, that the Kid can come out and play.

Looking at divergent thinking from the point of view of the packing example we described, it is fairly obvious that when Pamela suggested, "Why don't we just poke their eyes out," she had her Judge well under control. Someone else might have had that notion but decided it was a dumb, disruptive comment and kept quiet. And Frank, who suggested that they hire the blind to do the job, had his Judge diverted as well, for had he been there, the Judge would have quickly ruled the first suggestion out of order and called for the next idea.

Divergent thinking is important *just because* it is out of order or seemingly unrelated to the subject. It is this kind of thinking which shakes loose new perspectives, new ideas, and opens the "possibility" when logic tells us there is none.

Divergent thinking has a "loose" relationship with logic; it can, in fact, be quite illogical. It is the kind of thinking children do without self-consciousness, and which adults write off as childish. When your daughter tells you her best friend is living in her stomach, or your son describes how he flew his bed out the window and into the tree across the street, this is divergent thinking in its purest, most uncensored form. For the child, the Judge has not yet been born, and so we find childhood a time of free and unfettered imagination.

In being creative, we need to recapture that child-like feeling and spirit. Being able to suspend the Judge until the appropriate time is essential to developing a wide (divergent) range of ideas with which to work. Once we have the ideas, we then use the Judge to help us evaluate them by guiding us to ideas which are ultimately useful and appropriate. However, if the Judge is allowed to be part of the process too soon, he restricts the flow of ideas and makes the whole procedure unproductive.

In dealing with business problems, it is important that we use all of our thinking mechanisms, that *both* the Kid and the Judge participate in the work, transcending the usual thought patterns which keep us bound where we are. To do this properly, we should pay attention to a few guiding principles.

Alternate

Since we cannot use the Judge and the Kid at the same time, we must deliberately separate them from each other. Let the Kid do his thing — divergent thinking — then let the Judge do what he does best — convergent thinking. Combining them is like turning hot water and cold water on at the same time. What we get is luke-warm material, too weak to do us any good.

Diverge Then Converge

The more ideas and notions we have to consider, the greater the chance that a new, valuable insight will present itself. To make this happen, we must diverge first and invite *all* ideas and thoughts into the game. Only after we have exhausted our supply of logical, illogical, and ridiculous notions do we let the Judge decide from all the different options.

23

If You Think It, Write It

In much the same way that psychologists tell us to write our dreams down immediately upon waking, lest they be lost, we must do the same when we are in a divergent thinking mode. So, if you think it, write it down. Unrecorded thoughts tend to obstruct the free whimsical expression of the Kid's thinking process. Mental energy and attention which could be used to generate more ideas is spent trying to remember unrecorded ideas. Recording your ideas lets you clear the mental pipes, keeping the thought passages unobstructed and ready for the next idea.

Manipulate

Making Something

① *Larger* ④ *Considering it from a different point of view*

② *Smaller*

③ *adapting it*

Another powerful technique for greatly influencing the quantity and quality of your output while doing divergent thinking is to use Manipulation.

Creating always involves a manipulation of some sort. We take what exists and reshape or recombine it into a different configuration to solve a problem. Everything else is some addition or modification to what we already have. In being creative, there are only four ways to change things:

1. Make something larger, greater, or extend it.
2. Make something smaller, delete it, or miniaturize it.
3. Rearrange it, adapt it, transpose it, or substitute for it.
4. Consider it from a different point of view.

All innovation uses one or more of these four basic manipulations.

Trying Your Hand

Freely generating lots of ideas is not as easy as it sounds. We are all so accustomed to the authoritative voice of the Judge, we have come to obey, which means holding the Kid in check, without even thinking about what it has to offer. To help you break some of those barriers and free-up your thinking process, we have included a couple of exercises here, with additional, increasingly challenging exercises in Appendix A.

Before beginning, you will need a pad of paper, a pencil, and a watch or clock. Be disciplined about the suggested time for each exercise. As your skill increases, you will find yourself able to generate more and more ideas within a given amount of time.

> Take a look at the telephone on your desk, then list all of the ideas you can think of in ten minutes for making it more functional *in any way*.

A good score for this exercise would be twenty-five ideas. If you got less than twenty-five, don't worry, there are probably several things blocking you. For instance, you may have only been looking for good ideas.

Don't look for good ideas! At this point, any idea will do. It is only natural when you are trying to develop ideas, to want to find *the* idea, you know, the one which you will sell for a million-five so you can buy that condo on the shore. But what happens is that while the Kid generates ideas, the Judge evaluates each one as it appears, hoping it is *it*. And when it isn't *it*, the notion gets discarded. Then, after a few rejections, the Kid isn't having much fun, he loses interest in the whole activity, and the process shuts down.

Or another problem might be that you get an idea which has nothing whatever to do with a telephone. For example, your first thought might be, "Maybe I can improve the dial tone." Your next thought might be, "I've run out of Dial soap. I've got to remember to stop at the store on my way home." The Judge deems the second thought unrelated to a telephone, so it goes unrecorded.

As a matter of fact, the most insidious part of this whole process is that you censor so much and so often that you are not consciously aware of it happening. The cure is to *write down all thoughts*. It doesn't matter what they are about. If you think it, write it. Don't bother censoring it, just write it down.

Another way to capitalize on "inappropriate thoughts" is to consider using the thought to generate another, more relevant thought. For example, a thought sequence might go:

1. Improve the dial tone.
2. Go to the store to pick up more soap.
3. Have phones for purchase in grocery stores.

Allow yourself to associate freely when you wish to use Divergent Thinking. Let one thought lead to the next, regardless of where it takes you. In this way, all thoughts can be appropriate, and you are more likely to record them all.

> Looking at your "bookmark," in ten minutes, list as many ways as you can to get the most out of reading this book.

(Additional suggestions for practice appear in Appendix A.)

SKILL TWO — FORCING RELATIONSHIPS

Whether it is the artist sculpting new insight into visual form, the scientist discovering new techniques for improving a product, or the business person developing an innovative marketing plan, the creative process is the same. It involves at its core the ability to connect two or more apparently different ideas, concepts, or things which have been previously unrelated. This part of the creative process is called *Forcing Relationships*.

To some extent, we are all creatures of habit. We receive a stimulus and we respond automatically. This is the way most relationships exist for us. It is hard to think of Fred Astaire without thinking of Ginger Rogers. Try thinking of bacon without thinking of eggs. In the same way, because we work with many of the same people and circumstances day after day, certain thinking becomes almost automatic for us.

Unfortunately, that automatic thinking, while comfortable, is not always the most productive for getting us fresh ideas. To change our point of view, we must discover new, non-habitual relationships. We make these relationships by finding common elements in seemingly uncommon comparisons.

An example of a forced relationship would be a new car and an excellent marketing organization, or an iceberg and an effective manager. Although seemingly unrelated items, if you think about a new car or an iceberg, you can find characteristics and qualities which might also relate to excellent marketing organizations and effective managers.

New cars are tight, for example, every part fits and they don't rattle over bumps. Excellent marketing organizations are equally tight, with everyone doing their job without a lot of sloppiness. An excellent marketing organization does not rattle and shake when it encounters bumps, but absorbs the shocks and keeps on going.

An iceberg takes a long time to become an iceberg, usually breaking off a glacier after hundreds of years. Once spawned, the iceberg moves calmly but deliberately. Effective managers also take years to develop, and move their organizations with the same quality of deliberate calmness.

If we took the time, we could find many, many more qualities in common for each of these examples. This should, however, give you some idea of the kinds of relationships possible with this technique.

Forcing Relationships is one of the most powerful and productive creative skills we use in our consulting. It successfully stimulates new insights for our clients time after time. The following example is designed to give you experiences with Forcing Relationships, the best technique for working with them, and an understanding of how they can lead you to creative breakthroughs.

To help you, we will guide you through the first section step-by-step.

Suppose you are considering hiring an administrative assistant to alleviate some of your work load, and you want to minimize any organizational problems the addition might cause. See how long it will take you to develop ten ideas for minimizing complications by comparing your hiring process to an elephant. That is, how might considering an elephant help you to minimize organizational complications when you hire an administrative assistant?

A. Create Forced Relationship Form

Draw a line down the center of a full sheet of paper, making two columns. Over the right column, the "Insight Column," write whatever it is you are comparing *to* or what you want insights for. In this example, since you are looking for insights into your hiring process, you might label it, "HIRING PROCESS." Eventually, this column will contain a list of insights for hiring your administrative assistant.

(Key Column) ELEPHANT	(Insight Column) HIRING PROCESS

Label the left column (we will call it the "Key Column") with whatever you are using to unlock the insights. In this case, you are using an elephant to make the comparison so you might label it "ELEPHANT." Eventually, this column will contain a list of qualities and characteristics of an elephant.

B. Fill-In Key Column

Instead of trying to find relationships right away, concentrate only on the key column, in this case, the elephant. List as many descriptions or characteristics as possible, paying attention to, but not being limited by, the following two considerations:

1. Try to find descriptions that are phrases instead of a single word. For example, "runs in a pack" or "has a big trunk" will be more helpful than "big" or "gray." (However, don't leave the one word descriptions out.)

2. Try to find descriptive phrases which are more specific to elephants than to general objects. For example, "performs in a circus" and "tusks of ivory" are traits specific to elephants that are not characteristic of too many other objects.

The following is a list of characteristics for the elephant which you might find helpful.

(Key Column) ELEPHANT	(Insight Column) HIRING PROCESS
1. Big 2. Gray 3. Performs in circus 4. Tusks made of ivory 5. Dies in elephant grave yard 6. Has long trunk 7. Is really king of beasts 8. Has close family unit 9. Trumpets its sound 10. Is the largest land mammal 11. Was almost made extinct by hunters	

C. Fill-In Insight Column

Finally, develop the associations or connections with the insight column (minimizing risk in your hiring process) by considering each of the characteristics separately and finding at least one, but hopefully more than one, relationship for each. These are recorded in the Insight Column. If you make instant connections, feel free to write them down, or you might lose them.

(Key Column) ELEPHANT	(Insight Column) HIRING PROCESS
1. Big	1. Certify the new hire has a wide range of prior experience.
2. Gray	2. Look for someone who understands the subtlties and nuances of the business.
3. Performs in circus	3. Someone who presents themselves well.
4. Dies in elephant grave yard	4. Someone who is looking for a life-career with the company.
5. Has long trunk	5. Make transition time gradual.
6. Is really king of beasts	
7. Has tusks of ivory	
8. Has close family unit	
9. Trumpets its sound	
10. Is the largest land mammal	
11. Was almost made extinct by hunters	

Now you finish this example by adding insights of your own.

Almost anything can be used as a key to force relationships to your problem — baseballs, icebergs, Czarist Russia, radio talk shows — anything which evokes images in your mind from which you can pluck the details. You demonstrate the power and flexibility of this technique by using the same hiring problem, but trying a different key. You may get different insights.

Forcing relationships are difficult for some people when they start, because they are unaccustomed to thinking this way. But it becomes much easier with practice, and you will be amazed at how fluent and productive you can become.

Try the following:

Discover ten ideas for getting the most from this book by Forcing Relationships between maximizing your benefit (insight) and taking a cruise on a luxury liner (key).

(Additional suggestions for practice appear in the Appendix A.)

SKILL THREE — BECOMING THE ANGEL'S ADVOCATE

We think the following story accurately describes someone who understands the concept of becoming the Angel's Advocate.

An acquaintance who travels a great deal was at Chicago's O'Hare airport in a long line to check-in for a flight to Kansas City. The line was moving slowly, and he was hoping to have sufficient time for checking his luggage, when he heard an announcement over the loud speaker.

"Will passengers on American Airlines flight 206 to Kansas City please report to Gate 8."

Upon arriving at the gate with all of the other passengers, he heard an airline representative say, "Ladies and gentlemen, Flight 206 to Kansas City has been cancelled, the next flight is in five hours."

Needless to say, there were plenty of unhappy passengers, but out of the general groans of displeasure, our friend heard someone who was standing off to his right say, "Well, that's okay, I'm glad they cancelled it."

Curiosity piqued, our friend approached the trim, well-groomed businessman and asked what was so great about having the flight cancelled. The fellow looked at him for a moment and said, "Well, they cancelled the flight because there's something wrong with the plane, the pilot, or the weather. So in any case, O'Hare's just fine with me."

Our friend, who was momentarily taken aback said, "But they cancelled your flight! Didn't you have anything to do in Kansas City?"

The man responded, "Absolutely, a very important meeting, but we'll just have to have a conference call. Besides, if they're paying for it, the meeting won't drag on."

Our friend pressed his point, "Isn't this wasting your time?"

The man responded, "Well, you know I've always wanted to see the Museum of Science and Industry. Several people have told me it is wonderful. Now

I have time. The airline cancelled my flight. It is their airline, it is their prerogative. But they can't cancel my day!''

This story illustrates the fact that there are at least two sides to every problem. The first, and always the most obvious side, is that which wakes you at 2:30 a.m. with knots in your stomach. The problem eats at your stomach lining, producing anxiety, discomfort, and an ulcer!

The other side of a problem is less obvious and less often experienced. For every problem which produces discomfort and negative feeling, there are elements in it which need to be found and recognized. Quite often these elements are significant. For every roadblock or obstacle, there is a significant amount which is going right. The ability to find the positive potential in a problem is what we call becoming the Angel's Advocate, and the man in the airport was incredibly good at it. Instead of focusing on the unfortunate aspects of his situation, he found the positive opportunities it created for him.

Not all ideas are good ideas. We doubt that many people will find that a particularly profound or insightful statement. *But not all bad ideas are useless ideas, either.* Perhaps you will find that a little more profound, or at least enlightening, since most of us are in the habit of tossing bad ideas right into the dumpster, never to be seen again. Learning to become an Angel's Advocate means understanding how to look at a partially successful solution and separate the part that is useful from the part that is not.

To begin, think of ideas as existing along a continuum of value, an idea line which measures the worth of any idea for getting us where we want to go, like the following "idea scale," pioneered by Synectics Inc. of Cambridge, Massachusetts, and which we have adapted for our process.

IDEA SCALE

```
0      10     20     30     40 ................................................ 100
|       |      |      |      |                                                  |
```

Useless   Perfect

Assume that zero indicates the absolute pits of an idea, and conversely, 100 reflects something *better* than sliced bread. Now, if you are like us, you have probably never heard an idea that is 100. You can always find *something* wrong with every idea you have ever heard. To prove our point try the following exercise:

> In ten minutes, try to find as many things wrong with the following business truisms as you can.

>> "The customer is always right."
>> "Do it right the first time."
>> "If it ain't broke, don't fix it."

Just as you were able to find things wrong with ideas which on the surface look like 100s, it is possible to find things right with ideas that on the surface look like zeros. To do this, we can use Skill Two, Forcing Relationships.

For example, imagine that there has been a large turnover of your sales force over the last year, and you are looking for some new insights for developing the sales skills of your relatively young sales people. Look at the statement below. Using the Forced Relationship Form, we are going to step through the process of discovering what might be useful for learning salesmanship by looking at what is good about a weekly visit to the zoo.

"FOR DEVELOPING BETTER SALES SKILLS, EVERYONE SHOULD VISIT THE ZOO ONCE A WEEK."

A. Create Forced Relationship Form

Draw a Forced Relationship Form such as in the figure below.

(Key Column) Visiting the Zoo	(Insight Column) What's Useful for Developing Sales Skills?

B. Fill-in Key Column

Think of as many details and characteristics of the zoo as possible.

(Key Column) Visiting the Zoo	(Insight Column) What's Useful for Developing Sales Skills?
1. Zoos have many animals. 2. Many children go to the zoo. 3. The zoo is usually in a park setting. 4. Animals come from all over the world. 5. Animals are fed in public. 6. Zoos sell crackerjacks and soda. 7. We have to travel to get to the zoo. 8. Zoos have signs telling you about the animals.	

C. Fill-in Insight Column

Looking at each key, force a relationship between it and something useful.

(Key Column) Visiting the Zoo	(Insight Column) What's Useful for Developing Sales Skills?
1. Zoos have many animals.	1. We may learn about different consumers by watching different animals.
2. Many children go to the zoo.	2. We want our consumers as enthusiastic as children at the zoo.
3. The zoo is usually in a park setting.	3. We can learn more about the effect of our selling environment on people.
4. Animals come from all over.	4. Different approaches might be useful for customers of different backgrounds.
5. Animals are fed in public.	5. Perhaps we can invite our customers to lunch or dinner.
6. Zoos sell crackerjacks and soda.	6. We can learn more about consumer discretionary spending.
7. We have to travel to get to the zoo.	7. We can sponsor travel and trips for top salespeople and their families.
8. Zoos have signs telling you about the animals.	8. We can tell the history of our product on the box to let the packaging aid the salesperson.

Becoming the Angel's Advocate pays many benefits to those who master it. First of all, the Judge has no interest in finding value. An idea is either good or no good. So while you are looking for what is useful in an idea, you are neither accepting nor rejecting it. Looking for utility is the Kid's work and is therefore useful for promoting divergent thinking.

Second, because becoming the Angel's Advocate is a structure for exploring the most outrageous ideas, it lets you see what might happen in the next moment in time, or to consider the intermediate results of a notion. Considering the next moment in time often unlocks the new, useful part of an outrageous idea.

We can see how this works if we go back to the problem at the beginning of this chapter where the people were reading the newspapers when they were supposed to be packing the product in them. It was the consideration of the next moment in time, or the intermediate results that led them from "poke their eyes out" to "hire blind people."

If we think for a minute about the solution of "poke their eyes out," it is obvious that the intermediate results of poking their eyes out would be that the people would no longer be able to see. Their being no longer able to see is what would happen in the next moment in time. It is then a relatively short jump in the thought process to go from "no longer able to see" to "hire blind people." Exploring the next moment of the idea led us to a viable and practical notion with which everybody won. The following diagram shows what this thought process looks like.

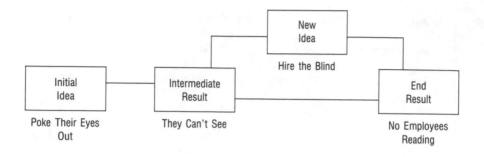

As you can see, "Hire the blind" was simply a different path to the same end result.

Here is another situation, taken from the Creative Problem Solving Institute, in which this particular technique solved a difficult problem.

A chain of stores in a large city was being plagued by a series of burglaries. The criminals responsible had a way of bypassing the burglar alarms, allowing them enough time to steal the merchandise between general police patrols. By the time the police got to the scene, the burglars had made their getaway with the merchandise. It was obvious that someone had to do something differently.

The store management defined the problem thus: "How can we help the police catch the thieves?"

After all the usual ideas came out about better, more expensive burglar alarms, someone suggested that the stores should be filled with gelatin in the evenings. Asked what would happen if the stores were filled with gelatin, the group concluded that it would be tough for the burglars to move around the store, thus slowing their getaway.

As soon as the idea of detaining the crooks was introduced, it was proposed that instead of lighting the stores at night, all lights should be off, keeping the stores in total darkness. Then they decided to rearrange the racks, eliminating a clear path through the store. These ideas were then coupled with installing light-activated sensors in the store to trigger a remote alarm as soon as the thieves turned on a flashlight.

The next time the thieves tried to burgle the store, they were so well detained, they were caught by the patrolling police.

Looking at our diagram again, we have:

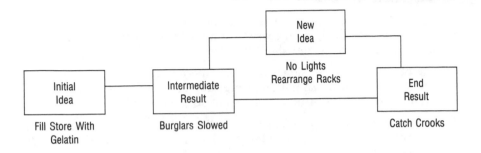

Just as you used the Forced Relationship technique to find what was wrong with good ideas, the technique can be used to find what is good in seemingly bad ideas. The process is exactly the same.

Step 1 — List the characteristics of the "bad" idea in the characteristics column. In the above example, you would record all the details and characteristics of filling the store with gelatin. Detaining the burglars is likely to be part of this list.

Step 2 — Look at each of the details and force a relationship between it and ways to catch the burglars. As you come to the detail which states that the burglars are detained, other, directly applicable ideas for detaining thieves spring forth. If you consciously consider the intermediate results, they often provide the key for taking a seemingly impractical idea and transforming it into something which works and yields some positive value for solving difficult problems.

Finally, one other important technique for using Forced Relationships to find value in ideas is to consider the implied meaning of the idea. When someone says, "Bill's all sizzle and no steak," they are obviously not comparing Bill with a piece of meat. What they are really saying, their implied meaning, is that while on the surface Bill is an impressive person, there is actually no real substance to him. Or, when considering a child's behavior, someone comments, "The seed doesn't fall far from the tree," they are not giving us a lesson in forestry. They are implying that to understand the child's behavior all we need to do is observe that of the parents. In other words, there are general implications which really concern themselves with the *intent* rather than the *content* of ideas.

If we consider the implied meaning of an idea or concept, as well as its literal content, it may provide us with ways of finding additional value in seemingly worthless ideas. Consider the following situation:

Several years ago, we were invited by a large, successful supermarket corporation to help them solve a shoplifting problem. After discussing the situation, two important facts emerged:

1. It seems that the great percentage of supermarket shoplifting generally involves items of little monetary value.
2. Shoplifting is treated as a misdemeanor.

This second fact meant that even when caught, the shoplifters would receive what amounted to a slap on the wrist from the local police department and were free to come back and shoplift again.

In one of the creative sessions with the supermarket managers, someone suggested that when the shoplifters were caught, their hands should be cut off. (Honestly, not *all* of our sessions are so violent.)

In the Forced Relationship exercise which followed, they examined the implied meaning of the "cutting their hands off" idea: *somehow increase the penalty for the crime.*

When the group then looked for ways of increasing the penalty, one of the facts we discovered was that the supermarket chain had recently installed a computer system to track inventories, supplies, production, and so forth. It was decided that when a shoplifter was caught for the first time, he would be told that he was no longer welcome in the store, and this information would be filed in the computer. This formal warning was legally necessary for them to be able to charge the criminal with trespassing if the person returned to shoplift.

The next time the criminal was caught shoplifting, he or she would no longer be charged with shoplifting but with the crime of "criminal trespassing," a felony and carried with it a much stiffer penalty.

Once again, we see how an idea that was seemingly ridiculous on the surface was modified and reshaped into something exciting, something which could be done, and something which went a long way towards alleviating a chronic, long-standing problem. Therefore, in finding value in ideas, it is important to place both "intermediate results" and "implied meaning" in the characteristics column of the Forced Relationship process.

How can some of these ideas and concepts help you in your work? Try the technique of finding value in the following exercise.

> You've generated a list of ideas for getting the most from this book. Now let your imagination go, and list the craziest, off-the-wall ideas for applying this book to your business. Finally, pick the most outrageous idea and use the Forced Relationship exercise for finding ten useful things about it.

In the detail portion, remember to include both the intermediate results and the implied meaning.

(Additional suggestions for practice appear in Appendix A.)

SKILL FOUR — DISSECTING IDEAS

You are now ready to experience the final skill and put to use all the opportunity thinking techniques you have tried in this chapter.

In Skill One, Divergent Thinking, you discovered the importance of the Kid, and of keeping the Judge under control, as well as how to allow one thought to trigger another. You practiced the art of manipulation, finding that one way of getting many thoughts or ideas for improving a situation or object is to describe it, then manipulate the description in terms of making something larger, smaller, rearranging it, or changing the point of view.

In Skill Two, Forcing Relationships, you solved problems by making associations or connections between two seemingly disconnected ideas.

In Skill Three, Becoming the Angel's Advocate, you used the first two skills to force relationships for finding value in seemingly impossible or ridiculous ideas. Two additional techniques for allowing us to find useful, positive characteristics, finding the intermediate results and identifying the implied meaning of an idea, were also introduced. These are helpful for finding potential opportunities in ideas that are not far enough along on our idea scale to use as is.

The Idea Scale Revisited

Reconsider the idea scale. In essence, the first three skills place an initial idea somewhere along the scale by determining all the useful things in it.

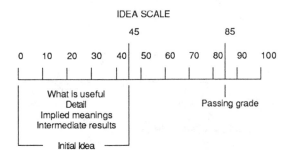

Assume that to consider using any idea, it must score at least 85 on the scale. This passing grade means we have great faith the idea will work, and we would be ready to implement the idea as is.

Imagine we have a situation where we have found all the value we can in an idea as it stands, and as far as we are concerned, it does not make a passing grade. Perhaps it is only worth about a 45. The gap of 40 points between an acceptable idea (85) and the present score (45) indicates *what is missing* in the idea. In other words, what is missing is all of the things we need to transform the idea from a 45 to an 85. By isolating what is missing in an idea, we can redefine the problem and expand our opportunities to resolve it creatively.

For example, suppose you are a manager in a medium-sized consumer goods business, and you see an opportunity to reduce cost and increase efficiency by installing a computer system. You might have no trouble finding value in this idea, and yet the idea might only be a 50 because you are missing some important things. One of them might be that you cannot get the approval for such an expenditure.

After all, setting up the system involves not only money for the hardware, but the software package would need to be customized for your application, and operators would need to be trained to use it. In other words, the gap is defined as all of those missing things that would make the idea good enough to be implemented with less than a 15% chance of failure.

The "How To. . ." Statement

The idea scale is dissected (or cut into parts) by any idea, the first part of which describes what is useful, while the rest identifies what is missing. What is missing becomes a new problem, and it is stated in a special way. The technique is to articulate the new problem with a statement beginning with the words "HOW TO. . ." Every time you talk about a problem, it should begin with these words. To illustrate, using the above example, the problem might be stated, "How to get the money to install the computer system."

Always begin with "How to...."

The problem which defines the gap in this example might be stated as "How to find the money?" Hence, to dissect an idea, one first develops a list of what is useful (employing the Forced Relationship techniques), and then defines what is missing with some "How to. . ." statements. Finally, one bridges the gap by generating ideas for the new "How to. . ." statements until the gap is closed. When the new idea, which is some modification of the initial thought, is at least worth an 85, it is ready to be implemented.

For the computer problem, some of the ideas we might get from the problem statement "How to find the money" would be:

1. Get another department to finance it.
2. Get a budget variance for the system.
3. Cut something else from your budget to pay for the system.

Assume that getting a budget variance looks the most promising, increasing the value of the idea from a 45 to a 60. The new gap is now defined as "how to get a budget variance." Repeating the process, we develop ideas such as:

1. Prepare a presentation for the boss.
2. Get the boss to think the idea for the system is his.
3. Go to your boss's boss with the notion.

Knowing your boss, the second idea looks like the best of the three. Repeating these steps, you finally close in on the 85 needed to give it a passing grade.

One last technique for using "how to" to redefine the problem involves changing the verb in the statement. For example, substituting other verbs for the word "find" we might get "How to steal the money. . .," "How to win the money. . .," "How to earn the money. . .," and "How to print the money. . ." One of these statements might have suggested some potentially valuable ideas that "How to find the money" did not.

It is time look at an overview of what we have done with the idea scale.

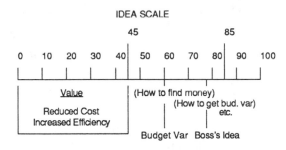

Therefore, through this repetitive process called the *floating problem statement*, we slowly close the gap by redefining the problem with "How to. . ." statements, until we find an idea which takes us to an acceptable solution.

Using the idea dissecting scheme, look at how the "poke their eyes out" idea was processed.

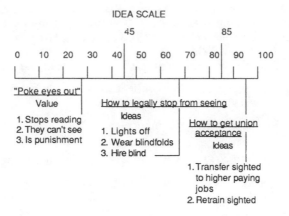

EVERYDAY PROBLEM SOLVING

It is easy to see how these four techniques, alone or in combination, can be effective for solving many of the daily problems you face. Simple problems seldom require a full-blown creative process to find innovative answers.

Think about some of the daily problems facing you right now. After identifying one, try using your new skills to find an interesting and/or unique answer. If you solve one right away, try another. If you don't develop a solution, you might want to carry the problem into Chapter Three, which deals with more difficult dilemmas.

A FINAL WORD

Elliot, a friend who is the creative director for a large advertising agency, had developed a wonderful advertising campaign for a major tire company. He had worked hard on the campaign and was looking forward to all the kudos he would receive and the increase in sales that the ad would mean. About four weeks before the ad was due to be filmed, he got a call from one of the attorneys at the agency who told him that he could not use the commercial because years ago something quite close to it had been aired by a competitor of his client.

Elliot was beside himself. Try as he might, he was unable to come up with anything that rivaled that great ad he had developed.

In his anguish, Elliot kept repeating to himself, "I'll never be able to come up with anything that good again." And then, one night at 3:00 a.m., he woke up with the answer.

About two months later, an ad campaign was aired by the tire company depicting an engineer in their research department being given a dinner by the company. His boss is shown giving a speech in his honor about the wonderful tire that the engineer had developed. At the end of the speech, the boss said to the engineer, "Now make it better." The ad closes with a flash of the engineer's anguished face saying, "I'll never be able to come up with anything that good again."

Elliot's story illustrates the fact that the core of the creative act is the continual redefinition of problems, so that the opportunities they hide present themselves.

Think about this poem by Richard Bach from *Illusions, The Adventures of a Reluctant Messiah*:

> There is
> no such thing as a problem
> without a gift for you
> in its hands.
> You seek problems
> because you need
> their gifts.

Can you become a seeker of problems? Can you find a way to look forward to them, to appreciate them for the opportunities they present for personal and professional success? If you can, you will be exponentially magnifying your potential and the potential of your business. With such a frame of mind, you will soon discover solutions sitting on your doorstep every morning.

Throughout the ensuing chapters, step-by-step techniques will be presented for solving the most difficult problems, selling their solutions, and implementing them. Each of these techniques will ask you to use the four skills you have explored in this chapter: Divergent Thinking, Forced Relationships, Becoming the Angel's Advocate, and Dissecting Ideas. They are the essential tools for honing and shaping ideas. With them, you can take the gifts offered to you by your problems and transform your company and your life into Innovation Inc. They are the tools for transforming dreams into experience.

Full Strength Problem Solving

A Problem-solving System for Resolving Difficult Business Issues

KALEIDOSCOPES AND CRYSTAL BALLS

Through the ages, crystal balls have been used in folk and fairy tales to look into the future. Gazing into the glass, the viewer sees clear pictures of what lies ahead: problems and pitfalls, perhaps, but most importantly, happy endings.

Often, problems are difficult to solve because our crystal ball is foggy, and we cannot tune in a clear picture of the happy ending. We don't know where we want to end up, and the picture is just too fuzzy to understand what the future will be like with the problem solved.

Creative thinking is the ability to take existing components and manipulate them into something new in order to solve a problem. The creative painter, for example, combines color, brushes, and techniques in a new way to express an idea (the problem) accurately. The creative package designer combines established blow-molding technology and container shapes to make new jelly and catsup bottles that won't make knives sticky or spurt catsup on the dress of the lady to the left.

Creative people often have a vision of what a solution might look like. They tend to think more in terms of the future, than the present. For them, "what could be" is more important than "what is." This sense of the future with the problem solved is essential, for the more nebulous and unexplored our notions of the future, the more we remain rooted in the present, and the more difficult it will be to make the changes necessary for innovation.

In a world where the only thing guaranteed to us is change, we must work to define and construct our own future. If we don't, someone else will define it for us — at our expense.

FULL-STRENGTH PROBLEM SOLVING

If you worked on a specific problem in the previous chapter and those techniques did not release the right kinds of solutions for you; if you feel you have a problem which requires a real breakthrough idea, a totally new way of looking at the situation; if you have a very long-standing problem that has been around the office for years, one of those you have "learned to live with"; you may need to use a process designed to take you even further from your normal thinking patterns.

Unfortunately, there are no simple answers for complex problems, no quick and dirty techniques for answering long standing, high-value problems in your business. It would be nice if there were, but there are not. Difficult problems demand more of the problem solver, and conquering them almost always requires concentrated time and energy. It takes hard work, very hard work. That's all there is to it.

It is for these more complex dilemmas that we created the process we call KALEIDOSCOPE. The process develops a very clear and detailed picture of the future with a successful solution being implemented, then helps you find pathways leading from where you are now into that desirable future. This process structures a variety of new techniques to stretch your imagination step-by-step, allowing you to consider your more difficult problems in new light.

KALEIDOSCOPE

Think about the infinite number of patterns and colors the kaleidoscope creates. With only three basic elements: light, colored stones, and a prism, a simple shift of any one element produces a stunning new pattern, each one unique.

Based on the principle of shifting elements, the Kaleidoscope process works by continually defining and redefining a future where successful potential solutions are being implemented. Disregarding the exact nature of the solution, it concentrates only on what is happening as a *result* of the solution's success. If we can get a very clear, very specific mental picture of what will happen because of a successful solution, it is likely that we can understand the kinds of changes needed to bring that picture to life.

Using the four creative skills — Divergent Thinking, Forced Relationships, Becoming the Angel's Advocate, and Dissecting Ideas — Kaleidoscope leads you through a step-by-step process for bridging the gap between a suitable future vision and a potential solution.

USING THIS CHAPTER

There are a variety of ways to use what follows in this chapter. You may wish to work through the process step-by-step with your unsolved business problem from the previous chapter. You may want to follow along as we relate our own example drawn from one of our clients. Or you may wish to read through it to get the main ideas behind the process. However you choose to use it, we believe you will find Kaleidoscope an exciting way to stimulate new and unique ideas for solving your more difficult dilemmas.

KALEIDOSCOPE — An Outline

I. Describing the Problem

    A. A brief description.

    B. What do you stand to lose?

    C. What have you already tried?

    D. What good is coming from the current situation?

    E. Summarize the problem with a "How to..." statement

II. Painting Future Pictures

    Assume a solution is being successfully implemented.

    A. Who is positively affected?

    B. Who stands to lose?

    C. The resource people.

    D. Raiding the Hall of Fame.

    E. Putting them all to work.

    F. What's exciting here?

    G. General Principles.

III. Using Analogies

    A. Parallel Worlds.

    B. Digging for Gold.

    C. Polishing for Perfection.

The problem solving model works in three sections. The first section, Describing the Problem, uncovers an initial opportunity in the current problem. Five questions ask the problem solver to identify the forces acting to perpetuate the problem, thereby uncovering the potential blockages maintaining the status quo. We spend little time considering the present situation. Rather than wallow in our present mess, we use the present as a resource to help us realize the future.

In the second section, Painting Future Pictures, we project ourselves into the future and assume we have solved the problem. We see ourselves busily engaged in implementing our solution.

Describing the successful implementation of a solution gives the problem solver a slight shift in attitude about the situation, making him or her feel more positive and excited about possibilities. This positive shift lubricates the imagination. Releasing new, positive energy into the situation makes it easier to escape from the current problem and find new perspectives. And by seeing ourselves implementing a successful solution, we create a series of divergent images which themselves provide the material for new ideas.

We begin painting our future by first developing a large list of people who might in any way be aiding the successful implementation. As the list lengthens, it diverges, finally including fictional and fantasy characters with unusual powers or abilities.

The people on the list become a super team, focusing all their skills and abilities on the problem, and we imagine vignettes describing what each person is doing. From these vignettes, we redefine the problem as an opportunity and perhaps discover a few new ideas for solving the problem.

In the third section, Using Analogies, we develop an analogy representing our successful resolution. The analogy allows us to examine our opportunity from a very different point of view. The new picture provides exciting, imaginative material leading to new ideas. The problem solver takes the most exciting of these ideas and removes the large obstacles for implementation by using the Dissecting Ideas skill from Chapter Two.

Kaleidoscope guides the problem solver through many different types of thinking in an intense, absorbing process. And although the process is structured by steps, the steps themselves are not always in a straight line. This creates opportunities for new patterns of thinking for people who tend to solve problems in an orderly, linear fashion.

If you get tired, or puzzled, take a break. Let your subconscious work for awhile, then come back refreshed with new perspectives. We believe you will find the ultimate rewards well worth the effort and concentration.

To demonstrate this process, we will move through it step by step, with an example from one of our consulting experiences. Although this particular example is in the manufacturing area, the process is the same for any business discipline. Don't be daunted if you work in a service industry, or if your problem falls within a non-manufacturing function. The specifics of this case are far less important than the steps taken to help the client resolve it.

The process is generic. We have used it successfully in large and small businesses of all kinds, in every business area. In the examples we use throughout the book, use the specifics to understand the process better and the kind of thinking necessary at any particular step. Then apply that thinking to your own problem.

THE EXAMPLE

PCP Corporation, a major manufacturer of baby diapers, is battling fiercely in both technology and marketing with its competitor, Robinson Products, the market leader.

Approximately a year and a half ago, Robinson developed and marketed a diaper with a new facing material which allowed liquid to pass through it while maintaining essentially dry contact with the baby.

In response, PCP's Research and Development Group produced a new technology based on advanced diaper facing research that had been done almost five years before.

Prototypes of the new diapers were quickly made on the research machinery, passing every lab test. These prototypes were also consumer-tested with great success against Robinson's diaper. Consumers preferred PCP's over Robinson's more than 60 per cent of the time.

Under normal developmental circumstances, PCP's R&D group would have next modified their research machine to run much faster, producing a far greater volume of facing material. This machine scale-up would have allowed them to anticipate and resolve new difficulties arising in the process from the greater speed and volume.

Such complications are common, and it is far easier to find and fix problems in a lab full of scientists, engineers, and analytical tools, than in a remote plant — especially when that plant is trying to meet its manufacturing quota at the same time. When problems arise while trying to test on a production machine, the lab needs to shut the machine down to figure out what is wrong, while the plant operators need to run the machine to meet their quota. World wars have started with less friction.

You can probably guess the rest of the story. Because PCP felt such pressure to get this new product into the market, they bypassed a scale-up of the research machinery to high-volume capacity. Instead, they went directly to a newly renovated, high-speed, high-volume commercial machine, and began the manufacture and marketing of the new diaper facing in huge quantities.

The operation was jinxed from the start. Thirty to forty percent of the time, the machine simply quit. When it did run, the product often failed the simplest quality tests. When the research engineers who had designed and built the lab machine were in the plant, the performance of the commercial machine improved, but as soon as they left, the operation went down the tubes.

Not surprisingly, the plant said, "it isn't our fault." They blamed the problems on a process which was not yet commercially viable. The research group, on the other hand, accused the plant of incompetence, claiming they did not understand how to run the machine. Regardless of blame, it became clear that a commercially viable technological modification had to be developed.

In the spirit of inter-departmental cooperation so prevalent in today's American corporations, the lab scientists agreed that they could fix it — in 18 to 24 months! Of course this time frame was totally unacceptable.

It was at this point that we were asked to help the lab develop ideas and action plans for dramatically shortening the time necessary to modify the process. Who was it that actually contacted us? It wasn't the Director of R&D. It wasn't the Director of Manufacturing. It was the Marketing Manager responsible for the diaper facing material who saw his sales numbers going down the drain while R&D and Manufacturing pointed fingers at each other.

With this as background, follow along as we describe how we used Kaleidoscope to help PCP find viable solutions to this problem.

I. Describing The Problem

A Brief Description

Begin with a brief (three sentences) conceptual overview of the situation causing concern. Using broad brush strokes, describe the current state, looking for a total overview in the most fundamental terms. The description is brief, simple, and to the point, and avoids dwelling in the present since we don't want our future to be influenced by it — since it might later limit our imagination.

PCP described their problem as follows:

> PCP, a manufacturer of diapers, has developed a new technology for a diaper facing material which allows liquid to pass through while leaving the surface dry. Although it has been a success in laboratory and market testing, the facing material is unable to be produced successfully in commercial quantities. We need to develop a technological fix and have it operational in six months.

> As you can see, the statement is succinct, and it does not
> particularly dwell on the negatives of the situation. It is a brief,
> balanced, and factual reporting.

What Do You Stand to Lose?

Recent studies show that people are more willing to risk change and
uncertainty *to avoid a loss* than to achieve a gain. Think about the last time
you played poker, when you knew you didn't have a winning hand, but you
had so much money in the pot, you were willing to risk more.

This phenomenon is easily seen in "me-too" corporations — companies which
lack the courage or insight to initiate innovation. Me-too corporations only
make changes once another company breaks new ground. When they see
market share eroding, the potential loss to the me-too becomes apparent and
risk becomes suddenly acceptable. They find themselves constantly catching
up with the latest technology, rather than initiating technological advances
themselves. The fundamental research and development for a me-too
corporation is done by their competition. Unfortunately, me-toos become
so risk adverse that when they try to innovate, they are sorely out of practice,
and they don't do it well.

Because the desire to avoid loss is the primary motivator for risking change,
we ask the problem solver to imagine all that might be *lost* if something isn't
done about the problem, rather than what stands to be gained by changing
the situation.

For PCP:

> We stand to lose a sizeable share of the market, from 15 to
> 20 million dollars per year, if something isn't done.

What Have You Already Tried?

Creative thinking requires a change in view because the original point of view
fails to solve the problem. But it is difficult to change a point of view if there
is not one in the first place. In other words, if the problem solver is not aware
of the limitations of the current situation, it is difficult to know whether or
not the limitations can be overcome.

The question checks several issues with the problem solver. First, to be sure
that some thinking and energy has already been put into the situation. Second,
it verifies that the problem solver really wants to resolve the issue. Many
times problems are not solved because the problem solver has some
subconscious vested interest in maintaining the status quo. Finally, if the most
logical and obvious solutions have not been explored first, then going through
Kaleidoscope may be a waste of time.

51

When we asked PCP, they said;

> We've tried to station our R&D people at the plant. When we do that, the operation gets slightly better, but when they leave, it slides back. We've also developed some "thought" experiments about modifying the technology, but everything we can think of takes a relatively long period of time.

What Good Is Coming From The Current Situation?

This question finds the forces that are maintaining inertia. Often, people do not make changes in apparently negative situations because in spite of the difficulties, they are still receiving something positive, too.

For example, a business associate, who is a key decision maker in a large corporation, continually complains about his company. He talks of updating his resume and moving to a more dynamic, futuristic, and flexible organization. Somehow, however, his resume still collects dust, and the status quo remains the status quo.

The explanation is simple. He also derives great satisfaction from his present position. His job is secure, he understands exactly what is expected of him, and he is compensated well for his time.

If we can make all the positive benefits of the current situation clear, then we can work to incorporate those positive benefits into any new solution we might develop. In this way, we minimize the potential loss any change might require and make it easier for the problem solver to change his point of view.

According to PCP:

> We (the R&D group) have a technical success, but the plant people are screwing it up so it doesn't have to withstand a final test in the marketplace. We've already gained awards for the new technology development, and stand to win more. We also stand to gain a higher budget because this situation makes it clear that R&D could perform even better if the decision makers expanded our funding and allowed us the time and resources to scale up the machines in R&D as we should.

> This statement was not quite as positive as we would have liked it to be. But this is how it came out. As you can see, it brings the friction between the R&D group and the plant very close to the surface, showing the apparent disregard the R&D people have for the competence of the plant people.

Summary

The summary is the first real attempt at creative problem solving. It takes all of the factors causing concern and problems and frames them into an opportunity. This is done with the use of the "How to. . ." statement. It allows us to look at a situation as being half-filled rather than half-empty. And it asks us to create an overall initial challenge that allows us to have our cake and eat it, too.

While going through the process, the "How to. . ." statement may change many times, but we are off to a good start by looking at the issue as creative challenges to be resolved, rather than as insurmountable obstacles keeping us mired in the present morass.

The statement the PCP group developed:

How to make the new diaper facing material a commercial success in six months or less.

Notice how this problem statement was quite a shift from the first one: "We need to develop a technological fix and have it operational in six months."

Initially, the group was trying to solve the technical problem. At this point, the group began looking to make the facing material a commercial success. At first they only considered the problem from a technical point of view. Now their view of the problem began to expand. While solving the technical problem may make the material a commercial success, the new definition allowed them to consider a wider range of solutions to arrive at the same bottom line.

II. Painting Future Pictures

Now it is time to travel into the future. Fueled with your powerful imagination, move forward in time to when a resolution to your problem is being successfully implemented. What is happening in this successful implementation? We are asking you to create mentally the *effect* of a successful resolution without considering *how* the resolution occurred. Once you have set your mind in the future, move on to the next question.

Who Is Positively Affected?

Ahh, the solution is being implemented, and working beautifully — even better than you thought it would, actually. Place yourself there with your imagination. Think about how good you feel having solved this problem. Then think about all the people benefiting from this solution. Try to consider as many people as possible who are gaining from your recent success.

Now is the time to let the Kid loose to do some Divergent Thinking. We are looking for a nice long list of people who may eventually become potential resources. A "people connection" exists in the solution to every problem. Even though a technical problem might require a machine to operate differently, or it might require a greater understanding of how to change a physical or chemical environment, nothing can be accomplished without people. Nothing.

In making your list, include people who may not be directly affected by the solution but may gain in some other way from the solution's ancillary benefits: family, friends, well-wishers, people in other disciplines who might gain from an indirect application.

Here is some of the list from the PCP case:

PEOPLE WHO STAND TO GAIN

1. Mothers
2. PCP marketing people
3. V.P. of R&D
4. Director of R&D
5. Lab employees in R&D
6. President of PCP
7. Plant manager
8. Plant quality control person
9. Machine operators
10. Plant person in charge of facing material
11. Plant director of operations
12. Spouses of plant personnel
13. Babies
14. Spouses of lab personnel
15. Fathers who work at home
16. PCP stockholders
17. Marketing person's secretary
18. Lab secretaries
19. Diaper sellers

> Actually, this is only a small fraction of the list they came up with. The longer the list, the better, and the more divergent, the better, too. At this point, don't inhibit your thinking in any way. Be as silly and farfetched as your Kid wants to be: Those ideas are important too. Do your best to hold your Judge at bay and let the Kid play around. The Judge will work soon enough.

Who Stands To Lose?

When there are winners, there are inevitably losers. Your share of the market comes out of someone else's. If there is one vice president and two directors, and one day the VP retires, someone is going to get the job, and someone is not.

However, a wealth of potential resources exists in all of those people who might resist or counter your solution in some way. People who we do not consider as being part of the solution but part of the problem can, with a slight change in perspective, provide the seeds for alternative solution paths that are simply never normally considered. Often, our clients have found potential solutions in the principle of "making your enemy your ally."

Remember, we are still living in the future, with the solution being successfully implemented. On a separate sheet of paper, develop another long list of people who in some way stand to lose by your success.

Here are some excerpts from PCP's list:

PEOPLE WHO STAND TO LOSE

1. The CEO of the competitor
2. Overtime workers at the plant
3. The airlines (R&D doesn't have to fly down to fix machine.)
4. Motel owners around plant (same reason)
5. The competitor's scientists
6. Assistant plant manager (won't get promoted by firing of his manager)
7. Assistant to the R&D director (see above)
8. The competitor's stockholders

One of the advantages of this section is that it starts the thinking processes looking for opportunities available in what appear to be the least likely circumstances. This is often the territory of innovation.

The Resource People

If your business were floundering and things were looking grim, wouldn't you like to call Lee Iacocca and say "Hey, Lee, gotta minute? I need a little advice." In fact, most problems have a variety of areas which would benefit by a whole panel of experts. You might need Lee for his management expertise, Paul Volker for his financial knowledge, and Apple Computer co-founder Steve Wozniak for his computer expertise.

This step in the process asks you to assemble your own panel of experts. Without restricting yourself to people to whom you have direct access, pick the world's experts. This is the time to think big. Be sure to break your problem into its component parts, and consider the best potential human resources to address each one. Notice in the following list that PCP considered interpersonal, moral, technical, and management issues.

PCP LIST OF EXPERTS

1. Lee Iacocca	5. NASA scientists
2. Japanese manufacturers	6. Dale Carnegie
3. Time management experts	7. Zig Zeigler (Motivational Speaker)
4. Steve Jobs (Computers)	8. Mother Teresa

Many difficult problems have varied and complex components. Be sure to examine yours from as many angles as possible.

Raiding the Hall of Fame

Now that you have considered all of the world's experts in the areas of your problem, it is time to move even farther into the imaginary world. The final panel of experts includes people fictional and real or who are no longer physically available. Search back through history and literature and find *three or four* people you would like to add to your panel of experts. Imagine being able to draw upon the experts through the ages: Superman or other super heroes, Sherlock Holmes, daVinci, or Einstein. Who would help you the most? Let yourself go.

Add Sherlock Holmes to your panel

The experts chosen by the PCP group were

> Franklin D.
> Roosevelt   Superman
> Sherlock Holmes   Lois Lane

Putting Them All to Work

If you are following along with the outline of the kaleidoscope model, we are at section II-E. At this point we develop another long list of activities these people are engaged in to aid in the successful implementation of this brilliant solution.

Each dot contributes to the total image

Here our crystal ball begins to clear. All the separate elements start to coalesce into something like a mosaic or a Pointillist painting, where each individual dot contributes to a larger picture.

This list of activities consists of one-sentence vignettes creating a mini-word-sketch of some positive occurrence having something to do with our desired future. Since each sentence should place us in a situation as if it were actually occurring today, use the present tense.

Creating these word pictures requires as much specificity as possible, therefore begin each sentence with the name of a specific person on your lists. Describe an action they are taking that is helping the successful implementation of the problem. What is it about that person that makes him or her unique? Try to use that special quality in your picture.

For an example of the kinds of statements we are talking about, look at the PCP case.

WHO'S DOING WHAT?

1. Mothers are purchasing large quantities of PCP Product.

2. PCP Marketing person is facilitating meetings between plant personnel and R&D to keep everyone focused on the marketing objective.

3. The VP of R&D is hiring an ad hoc task force of summer students to speed up the testing of the new R&D options.

4. The Director of R&D is inviting plant personnel to work at the R&D labs alongside the bench scientists.

5. The lab people have discovered an "easy way" to run the new technology in the mill.

6. The lab has developed robots to run the plant process to negate any chance for human error.

7. The President of PCP has both the plant and R&D reporting directly to him.

8. President of PCP is presiding over stockholders meeting, telling them about the new market inroads.

9. The plant manager is highly excited about the new technology process.

10. Plant manager is having informal dinners once a month with the R&D director.

11. The machine operators have developed quality circle groups to increase the learning curve for the commercialization of the new technology.

12. Machine operators have developed their own technology modifications.

13. Plant quality control person has developed techniques to speed testing of the commercial products.

14. Plant quality control person is spending more time on the machine and is able to equate product testing with machine runability.

15. Plant director of operations is learning how to run the machine.

16. Plant director of operations is promoting the machine operators because of efficiency breakthroughs they have made.

17. Plant person in charge of the facing material is spending more time in R&D.

18. Wives and babies of plant personnel are testing the new diaper facing and are providing immediate feedback to the plant.

19. Children of the plant personnel are performing menial tasks to free the plant operators so they won't have to think about things.

20. Spouses of the lab personnel have brought the bedrooms into the lab so lab people can spend more time at the bench while enjoying the benefits of home life.

21. PCP stockholders are voting for a greater share of the profits to go into research rather than dividends.

22. Marketing person's assistant has moved to the plant.

23. Lab secretaries are also doing lab experiments.

24. Supermarket owners are giving PCP products more facings and exposure on the supermarket floor.

25. The competitor's CEO is withdrawing its competitive product from the market.

26. The airlines are reducing fares for flying from the research facilities to the plant.

27. The airlines are putting a private plane at the disposal of the PCP plant personnel to fly to research whenever they want.

28. The airlines are showing films of the production process to R&D people on their flight to the plant.

29. Motel owners around the plant are putting in Nautilus equipment for use of the plant and R&D people.

30. Motel owners are supplying baby sitters for R&D families on their visits to the plant.

31. The competitor's scientists are leaving and joining PCP to help in the commercialization of the new technology.

32. Overtime workers at the plant are doing quality control testing instead of fixing the machinery.

33. The assistant plant manager is operating the machine when the workers take their break.

34. The assistant plant manager is taking courses at the local college in chemistry and chemical engineering.

35. The asst. to the R&D director is opening an R&D annex at the plant.

36. The competitor's stockholders are papering their living rooms with their now worthless stock.

WHO'S DOING WHAT?

---

37. Lee Iacocca is communicating his vision of teamwork to a joint meeting of the plant and R&D people.

38. Japanese manufacturers are setting up a training program for the hourly workers on the production line.

39. Time mgmt. experts are showing researchers how to truncate the time it takes to get results on their experiments.

40. Steve Jobs has developed an interactive program on the Apple that plugs the R&D homes into the plant mfg. site.

41. NASA scientists have miniaturized the production machinery so that a working model is on each lab bench in R&D.

42. Dale Carnegie is giving courses to all plant and R&D management personnel.

43. Zig Zeigler is supplying subliminal motivation tapes to all hourly employees in the labs and at the plant site.

44. Mother Teresa is having a "love-in" for all project members.

45. FDR is holding weekly fireside chats about the state of affairs in the mill and in R&D.

46. Sherlock Holmes is studying the fundamental causes of the discrepancy in performance between the lab and the mill.

47. Superman is transporting the production site to the R&D labs.

48. Superman's x-ray vision is determining the trouble spots on the machine.

49. Lois Lane is doing a weekly column on up-to-date performance data from the plant.

> In looking over these statements, notice how one idea or thought spawns another. Sometimes, one idea spins-off three or four others.

For the Kid, too much is not enough. Divergent thinking generates quantity, and that is the only criterion. The more ideas we have, and the greater the variety of ideas and notions, the better our chances of finding something which is truly unique.

Finally, it is equally obvious that the thoughts generated by the Kid are not all necessarily feasible. We simply have a picture of the future exactly the way we would like to have it. It is pure imagination. Feasibility is not a criterion. In fact, it would greatly hinder the process.

The value of these thoughts is less in the specific ideas than in their conceptual spirit. Like most precious commodities, ideas need to be refined; their usable qualities need to be extracted from the unusable, then highlighted, polished, and set. The remainder of the Kaleidoscope process accomplishes this work.

What's Exciting Here?

Finally, it is time to ask the Judge to make a few decisions. With such a specific, detailed picture of the future, we step back from the canvas and look at what we have. The common myth says that creativity is the process of getting unique ideas. But this definition does not tell the whole story. Creativity is also the process of finding value in the ideas you get and filling in the gaps which prevent them from being useful. When you have found a unique idea, evaluated it, and implemented it, then you have been creative.

So at this point, as we look over the long list of activities, we look for the ones with which we find some spark of interest. The idea need not be feasible at all — simply have something in it which, if it could be realized in any way, would be very exciting to you. Exciting is the important word. The thought should make you sit up a little, raise your interest quotient a point or two. That is the idea you want to mark.

There are two reasons for doing this. First, we will use the exciting items as stimuli for potentially productive, viable ideas by Dissecting them, looking for what is useful and what is missing; and second, we will try to look at them as a whole and see what they generally have in common. This is an inductive approach for discovering hidden opportunities by going from the specific (the action vignettes) to the general, which is discussed in the next section.

When we did this exercise with PCP, they picked the following as exciting items:

EXCITING IDEAS

---

3. The VP of R&D is hiring an ad hoc task force of summer students to speed up the testing of the new R&D options.

6. The lab has developed robots to run the plant process to negate any chance for human error.

7. The President of PCP has both the plant and R&D reporting directly to him.

11. The machine operators have developed quality circle groups to increase the learning curve for the commercialization of the new technology.

14. Plant quality control person is spending more time on the machine and is able to equate product testing with machine runability.

25. The airlines are reducing fares for flying from the research facilities to the plant.

30. The competitor's scientists are leaving and joining PCP to help in the commercialization of the new technology.

32. The assistant plant manager is operating the machine when workers take breaks.

36. Lee Iacocca is communicating his vision of teamwork to a joint meeting of the plant and R&D people.

39. Steve Jobs has developed an interactive program on the Apple that plugs the R&D homes into the plant mfg. site.

41. Dale Carnegie is giving courses to all plant and R&D management personnel.

44. FDR is holding weekly fireside chats about the state of affairs in the mill and in R&D.

47. Superman's x-ray vision is determining the trouble spots on the machine.

General Principles

What are all these details telling us? What do they add up to? How can we sum them up in a sentence? The idea here is to find one over-riding concept or principle which embodies the spirit of all these details. It enables us to step back from our fanciful immersion into the future state and see with an objective eye what new pathways and general tendencies are important to us.

A mosaic, up close, holds little real message for us. It isn't until we step back that we not only see the entire picture, but can also grasp the greater meaning and expression of the artist. The general principles are a leap to the next level of thought. And it is from that level that we will emerge with new, very specific, very viable and implementable ideas.

Reducing all these vignettes of the future to one general statement is a two-step process. The first step is to translate those chosen as exciting items into actual ideas for solving the problem at hand.

In the PCP example, we were looking for ways of making the diaper facing a commercial success in six months or less. Our challenge is to take the fourteen vignettes we identified as exciting and use them to get specific ideas for solving that problem. We do this using the Forced Relationship Technique discussed in Chapter Two.

If you are working your own problem through with us, draw a forced relationship form like the one below and list your "exciting items" in the Key Column. Then use those items to unlock specific ideas for meeting the challenge of your problem in the Insight Column.

(Key Column) Exciting Items	(Insight Column) How to make facing commercial success in six months or less.
The VP of R&D is hiring an ad hoc task force of summer students to speed up the testing of the new R&D options.	
Lab has developed robots to run the plant process to negate any chance for human error.	
The President of PCP has both the plant and R&D reporting directly to him.	
The machine operators have developed quality circles to increase the learning curve for commercialization.	
Plant Q/C person spending more time on machine, can equate product testing with machine performance.	
The airlines are reducing fares for flying from the research facilities to plant.	
The competitor's scientists are leaving and joining PCP to help in the development of the new technology.	
The asst. plant manager is operating machine during worker breaks.	
The asst. plant manager is taking local college courses in chemistry and chemical engineering.	
Lee Iacocca is communicating his vision of teamwork to a joint meeting of plant and R&D people.	
Steve Jobs has developed an interactive program on the Apple that plugs the R&D homes into the plant mfg. site.	
Dale Carnegie is giving courses to all plant and R&D management personnel.	
FDR is holding weekly fireside chats about the state of affairs at the plant and R&D.	
Superman's X-ray vision is determining the trouble spots on the machine.	
Increase number of people working in lab to free-up R&D people to work on more new things.	
Write an SOP manual which appeals to a poorly educated mentality.	
Make everyone on facing team responsible to one person.	
Encourage workers to give and implement ideas.	
Develop statistical relationships between machine settings and product quality.	

(Key Column) Exciting Items	(Insight Column) How to make facing commercial success in six months or less.
Develop special contracts with airlines for plant/R&D round trips. Hire former employees of competitor to learn their commercialization policies. Management coverage on all three shifts instead of just first. Educate plant management personnel in new technology skills. Hold general mtng of all employees on the facing to emphasize single vision. Widen the pipeline of information from R&D to plant and back again. Have all managers learn sales and interpersonal skills. Weekly communications briefings with conference calls for all concerned employees. Bring high-tech research diagnostic equipment to the plant to analyze existing problems better.	

Now it is time to look at the exciting items in the left column as a whole. If you can, put them in one place where you can easily see them all and allow your eyes to scan from one to the other. What kinds of general impressions are you getting? Allow a fuzzy image to surface in you. You should, with a little work, come up with one or two sweeping statements of one sentence which have within them all the specific ideas for capitalizing on your opportunity.

For PCP, the general statement was this:

> All the people associated with the facing project are working more closely together, each helping the other to accomplish their tasks with increased communication and cooperation.

This is quite a distance from the problem we began with, which involved the development of a new laboratory technology. But then again, problem solving involves the redefinition of the problem in such a way that solutions present themselves. This describes the evolution we went through with PCP, as well as the evolution of all problems.

Save the paper with the ideas you have just generated. We will hold them on the side for now and bring them back later.

III. Using Analogies

Parallel Worlds

Next we develop a list of opportunities from which we will create the events leading up to implementation. We do this by finding analogies to other situations in life which operate by the same general principles. We call these other situations parallel worlds.

For example, we might look for an analogy in the world of religion, sports, or the Wild West. Which "world" does not matter, as long as it offers examples which are analogous to the general principles. However, in selecting a world, it is important that it be remote from the world of the problem. A business analogy for a business problem is too close, while a comparison to the world of TV sitcoms or meteorology might be more fruitful.

How can this .... help this?

The world you select should also be something you know a little about, and finally, you should be able to pick a specific event, moment, or example which epitomizes that world. The "1927 New York Yankees" would be a better selection than simply "World Champion Baseball Teams." Since you are going to record as many details as possible about the analogy, it needs to be clear and specific.

The following list of "worlds" will get you started, but feel free to use your own if you prefer.

PARALLEL WORLDS

American Literature	Geography	Photography
Animal Kingdom	Geology	Physics
Architecture	Gourmet Food	Politics
Art	Great Documents	Pornography
Astrology	Great Religious Books	Psychology
Astronomy	Insects	Revolutionary War
Biology	Inventions	Shakespeare
Bowling	Journalism	Soap Operas
Comics	The Jungle	Social Movements
Composers	Law	Space
Computers	Liberation Movement	Television Sitcoms
Dance	Machines	Tennis
Economics	Manufacturing	Theatre
Education	Medicine	Transplants
Electronics	Meteorology	Transportation
Entertainment	Monuments	Vietnam
Evolution	Movies	Wild West
Finance	Mysteries	Wine
Fishing	Mythology	WW II
Flying	Nutrition	
Football	Philosophy	

It is best to look for three or four worlds, then pick that one which is the best representative of your general principle. For PCP, they finally chose the world of hockey, and their example was the 1980 U.S. Olympic Hockey Team.

Digging For Gold

Now we begin hunting for valuable information embedded in our analogy. In the case of PCP, we will look at as many aspects of the 1980 Olympic Hockey Team as possible. We explore all sides and surfaces looking for information which might unlock ideas for solving our own dilemma. Our principle tool is the Forced Relationship.

This is another divergent episode where we allow the Kid to play with the analogy and list as many details about it as possible. Try not to censor him or shut him down in any way: all notions are good and are eligible for the list. This divergence is important because we are going to use these statements to stimulate ideas for solving our own analogous situation, and we cannot tell ahead of time where that breakthrough idea will come from.

Look at some of the information PCP listed about the 1980 U.S. Olympic Hockey Team.

(Key Column) 1980 U.S. Olympic Hockey Team	(Insight Column)
1. Team had strong coach. 2. There was a designated "whipping boy." 3. They played against pros to practice. 4. They were representing the U.S. 5. There was an abundance of talent. 6. They took advantage of all the small breaks. 7. They didn't think they could be beaten. 8. Olympic games were at home. 9. Didn't want to look bad before the home crowd. 10. Someone picked up slack if mistakes were made. 11. Players were better skilled because of increased emphasis in their younger years.	

Using these elements as keys for unlocking ideas, the following diagram shows some of the notions PCP got by allowing these details from the 1980 Olympic Hockey Team to stimulate ideas for getting people to work more closely together.

(Key Column) 1980 U.S. Olympic Hockey Team	(Insight Column) How to get people to work closer, and to help each other. . .
1. Team had strong coach.	1. Provide ad hoc decision maker for the whole group.
2. There was a designated "whipping boy."	2. Show group how competition was willing to "take bread out of their mouths."
3. They played against pros to practice.	3. Scale research machinery up to plant speeds.
4. They were representing the U.S.	4. Identify facing as a PCP project, not plant or R&D.
5. There was an abundance of talent.	5. Hire bright summer students to work in the plant.

(Key Column) 1980 U.S. Olympic Hockey Team	(Insight Column) How to get people to work closer, and to help each other. . .
6. They took advantage of all the small breaks.	6. Make careful study of all parameters when commercial machine makes acceptable product.
7. They didn't think they could be beaten.	7. Have a pep talk or rally for team by CEO of PCP.
8. Olympic games were at home.	8. Relocate the laboratory in the mill environment.
9. Didn't want to look bad before the home crowd.	9. Have President and CEO visit the plant regularly.
10. Someone picked up slack if mistakes were made.	10. Train people in the duties of more than one job. Train machine operators in chemistry.
11. Players were better skilled because of increased emphasis in their younger years.	11. Interdepartmental lectures by scientists to plant people to educate them. Lectures about plant philosophies to R&D group.

As you can see in numbers 10 and 11, two ideas were spawned by the keys in the left hand column. Using metaphors is a very powerful technique for finding new and exciting concepts. They allow you to think about the problem in new ways and from totally different points of view.

If you would like more ideas of a different nature, or if you find that the ideas generated the first time were not very useful, try again with a different metaphor. Different metaphors almost always generate slightly different potential solutions.

Now we have a lot of raw, undeveloped, potentially implementable solutions. Not only do we have the ideas we just generated with the metaphor and forced relationships, but we also have the ideas for commercialization in six months that we put aside earlier.

Polishing For Perfection

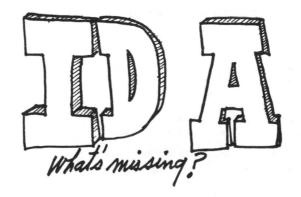

If you are working on your own problem, take all your ideas and put them where you can see them. Look them all over carefully and weigh their value to you in taking you toward the solution to your problem. It is time to pick those with the best potential, shine them up, and remove the imperfections.

The polishing process is done using the coarsest sandpaper initially, removing the largest, most obvious obstacles first. This section is designed to accomplish that initial heavy-duty work. Later chapters address the fine tuning necessary for actual implementation.

Begin by finding the single most promising of all the ideas, and then remove the obstacles preventing it from being an implementable idea. Draw on the technique of Dissecting the idea, looking for what is useful and what is missing from making it immediately implementable.

It is important to remember that once all the obvious blockages are cleared away, other work still remains before it is time to implement. It is also possible that we will come across a roadblock or a what is missing statement that we simply are unable to bridge reasonably. Don't worry, there are techniques for those situations in the next chapter.

When PCP came to this point in the process, they decided to combine several of their ideas into one. They decided to move a substantial portion of the R&D effort to the plant site, changing the focus from developing a new R&D technology to understanding why the present technology was making trouble. They then decided to institute quick fixes with the help of all the plant people who had been involved in the material's development. That is the idea they decided to develop with the following steps.

What's useful

A. There is a greater opportunity for short-term success since they would be working under real conditions.

B. This solution promotes increased understanding, communication, and cooperation from everyone involved.

C. This solution expands skills, attitudes, and improves morale by incorporating many disparate points of view.

What's missing

"How to move the R&D effort to the plant and minimize the relocation problems?"

Next, they began a brief brainstorming session for solving this latest "How to. . ." The four ideas which follow were among the many they generated:

✓1. Use space in the plant's quality control laboratory.

✓2. Lease as much lab equipment as possible from a local supplier at the lab site.

✓3. Develop a generous travel package for families.

4. Enlist the aid of professional movers as consultants.

A combination of ideas 1, 2, and 3 seemed to minimize the problem successfully. The check marks indicate an idea that was chosen.

What's useful in the idea

A. The plant space is currently available and unused.

B. It minimizes the amount of material which has to be transported to the plant from the R&D facility.

C. It minimizes concerns about being separated from families for extended periods of time.

These solutions seemed to take them far along their way to a course of action, but there were still some concerns which needed to be addressed.

What's missing in the idea

"How to focus, organize, and administer the work of the plant site and the lab personnel?"

Two of the ideas they generated were:

✓1. Appoint an ad hoc team of two people (the assistant plant manager and the assistant research director) as the decision making body located in the plant.

2. Appoint a marketing person to head the cooperative group in the plant.

Of these two, they chose number one to mitigate their concern about focus, organization, and administration.

What's useful in the idea

A. Two different points of view would yield better decisions.

B. Cooperation between the plant and R&D would be instituted from the top down.

C. Each person on the team would have someone on the decision-making team to identify with.

What's missing in the idea

"How to maintain an R&D effort towards future new product and process development back at the R&D site, when so many of the people will be down at the plant."

The ideas

✓1. Hire summer students.

✓2. Have an R&D/Plant exchange program for plant people not engaged in the diaper liner project.

✓3. Farm some R&D work out to the local university.

4. Defer some new product development thrust until the diaper liner problem is resolved.

They decided on a combination of ideas 1, 2, and 3.

What's useful about this idea

A.   Plant people will expand their horizons.

B.   New jobs will be created for young, potential employees.

C.   New points of view will be brought to research problems.

What's missing in the idea

"How to get commitment from everyone potentially involved in the implementation process."

The answers to this final problem, gaining acceptance for a new idea, will be developed later in the book. This can be one of the most critical areas for actually accomplishing something. Often, brilliant ideas are conceived and developed, only to be shot down by others with greater power or authority. Selling ideas is such a critical area, it deserves a chapter by itself.

Summary

Now that you have been through it in detail, take another look at the whole process in outline form on the following page. Think quickly through the problem you followed. Try to get an overview of the total flow.

You have just been through a complex process for solving very difficult problems. It is an idea management system which reserves time for both the Kid and the Judge, while keeping them out of each other's way. It is also a process which forces you to exercise your imagination. This is not necessarily the process you might use to develop ideas for reallocating office space. The process demands time and concentration, so reserve it for problems which are worth that investment.

As a final word, don't feel that because there is a process outlined here, that the process can't be modified or changed. In fact, we encourage you to adapt it to your needs. Don't allow yourself to become a slave to the system. It is there to work for *you*, feel free to take it and make it your own.

KALEIDOSCOPE — An Outline

I. **Describing the Problem**

    A. A brief description.

    B. What do you stand to lose?

    C. What have you already tried?

    D. What good is coming from the current situation?

    E. Summarize the problem with a "How to..." statement

II. **Painting Future Pictures**

Assume a solution is being successfully implemented.

    A. Who is positively affected?

    B. Who stands to lose?

    C. The resource people.

    D. Raiding the Hall of Fame.

    E. Putting them all to work.

    F. What's exciting here?

    G. General Principles.

III. **Using Analogies**

    A. Parallel Worlds.

    B. Digging for Gold.

    C. Polishing for Perfection.

Selling Your Solutions

How to Gain Support
for Making an Idea a Reality

The person who follows the crowd, will usually get no further than the crowd. The person who walks alone is likely to find himself in places no one has ever been before.

Creativity in living is not without its attendant difficulties, for peculiarity breeds contempt. And the unfortunate thing about being ahead of your time is that when people finally realize you were right, they'll say it was obvious all along.

You have two choices in life: you can dissolve into the mainstream, or you can be distinct. To be distinct, you must be different. To be different, you must be what no one else but you can be. . .

— Author Unknown

An exhilarating, magnificent feeling electrifies both body and soul when we grasp a breakthrough, a new perception, a new discovery, a new idea. It may happen while trying to identify a problem, when the gaps between the present and future state unveil themselves, while brainstorming, or even while standing in the shower after thinking about a problem for three days. Whenever it strikes, it is powerful. We are awed by the simplicity of the insight challenging us. We are different. We stand alone with our idea. We are our idea. And it is good.

So what do we do? We tell someone about it. We want them to see, to feel, to experience our creativity. We want their world to be different because of it. At this moment, nothing is more important than sharing this incredible notion. So in one swift motion you snatch-up the telephone or rush into a colleague's office. You interrupt an annual review meeting, but you don't care. The idea is worth it. The idea will get you by. So there you stand, flush with excitement.

"Jack, I got an idea."

"Jill, uh, I'm in a meeting right now."

"Jack, it's a big one. Really big. You want to hear it?"

"Actually, Jill, I want to give Bob, here, his performance review. Come back in about forty. . ."

You cut him off, "Just let me tell you. Please. . ."

Bob, who didn't like the way his review was going anyway, is just as pleased to delay the bad news. "Go ahead, Jack, I don't mind," he says, "it'll just take a minute."

Jack pauses, sits back, invites you with his silence to divulge your great secret. He's waiting. You take a breath. You tell him. It's simple. It's sweet. It's direct.

Jack pauses, as if he is expecting more. Suddenly he sits up, "That's it?"

You nod, uncertain of his reaction.

"We can't do that. We don't have the budget for it. Who's going to pay for it?"

"But Jack," you say, incredulous.

"I didn't think it was such a great idea either," says Bob.

"Look," says Jack, "I don't want to disappoint you, but Benson had that idea eighteen months ago and couldn't find anyone to pay for it."

You are speechless. Benson was fired last year for sexual harassment. Everyone knew he was a jerk. You slink out of Jack's office, back to yours. In retrospect, even you think it's a bad idea now. And you wish you had never had it.

People like predictability, but new ideas mean change. It isn't really you they object to. . . it is the change your new idea suggests. A colleague of ours refers to creativity as "overcoming your own conditioning." This implies that when you invite someone to accept your new idea, you also ask them to be creative, to overcome their own conditioning. For most people, this is very difficult. They may not be used to thinking creatively. They may lack the imaginative flexibility to see all the value you find in the notion. They may just not be in the mood at the time you tell them. Regardless of the reason, rejection can be devastating to an idea, as well as to the person who had it. So what do we do?

most people resist change . . . !

We can "dissolve into the mainstream," forgetting about breakthroughs, or we can "be what no one else can be" — an initiator, an innovator, and use that creativity to help us insure our ideas get implemented.

If you want to turn an idea into a reality, two questions must first be answered:

- Do you own the idea enough?
- Do you own the idea enough to let go of it?

do you own an idea?   *Can you let go of it?*

To answer yes to both questions sounds paradoxical, yet those two yeses lie at the heart of getting what you want. By living those polarities, you become distinct, different, unique.

DO YOU OWN THE IDEA ENOUGH?

Once you have an idea, how important is it to you? Three aspects of ownership determine if the idea is important enough to you to implement: vision, personal commitment, and authority.

Vision

Vision is seeing your idea as a reality. Edison must have seen a room full of light; Picasso, a completed canvas; Lincoln, freedom from oppression; Disney, a magic kingdom. A vision may be the sound of a choir of trumpets, the touch of chipped and polished marble, the fragrance of fresh-from-the-oven bread, a new concept of a micro/macro-universe, or the harmony of a winning team. Though the specific steps to get there may be obscure, the vision of the end must be clear. It stands before you, teasing you, obsessing you. You know it is possible, somehow. You feel it. You taste it. It exists for you viscerally, in some way. Its reality is almost tangible. A vision is a conscious dream.

Personal Commitment

Are you willing to put yourself on the line? Personal commitment says that this idea is important enough to invest my valuable time and energy in it.

Many good ideas lose momentum after a night's sleep because we wake up newly aware of the work and the obstacles which will have to be overcome if we attempt to implement our idea. That is when you say, "Well, it was a good idea, but I just don't have the time. . ." Or we may give up midstream, discouraged and disappointed in ourselves, having discovered we have underestimated the personal energy required. From the onset, we must be willing to determine realistically our desire to give what it takes to see the idea through.

Authority

Authority is easy — and hard. It requires the participation of one person, you. You simply acknowledge to yourself, sincerely, with vision and personal commitment, that you can do it. Ultimately, you do not need permission from your boss, your spouse, your parents, or anyone. Authority comes from within. No one can take it from you. And when you grant it to yourself, fully, you will make your idea come true. Without self-granting authority, however, it will be very difficult to implement the idea. It is easy — and it is hard.

When we make ourselves the victims of others' authority, we remain dreamers, not doers; followers, not leaders; mainstream, not slipstream. Denying authority is one of our favorite ways of limiting ourselves, of shirking responsibility for inaction. Naturally, some ideas are more easily implemented when we have the power of an office in the organization, decision making responsibility for budgetary expenditures, and personal clout. But true empowerment comes from *within*.

With a vision to inspire you, a commitment to drive you and self-granted authority to support you, "you own the idea enough."

DO YOU OWN THE IDEA ENOUGH TO LET GO OF IT?

Our ideas are not us. That is easy to say, and difficult to believe sincerely. More often our ideas are grafted directly to our egos. They form an inviolable alliance with our sense of self. An attack on one is an attack on the other. Such an arrangement drives many individual efforts to successful conclusions, but individual efforts are exceedingly rare and difficult to achieve in business.

To implement ideas successfully in the business environment, to be creative to the very end of the process, we must somehow interact with others. And that means we must find a way to divorce our ideas from ourselves.

Few of us will ever have statues erected in honor of our good ideas, at least in our own lifetimes. In fact, weeks, months, years, decades, or even centuries can pass between the inception of an idea and its reality. Ideas come in a flash but new realities, new ways of doing things, or new products take time for acceptance. When we are ahead of our time, we can wait until others see our ideas as obvious, or we can choose to make the strange familiar. We can make our breakthrough a breakthrough for others. To do that, the idea must be understood, accepted, and then owned by them.

Weeks, months, years, even decades may pass between the inception of an idea and its reality.

You may know who invented the light bulb, but do you know who discovered organic light, or who invented glow in the dark digits for watches? You may use Post-its, you may even know that 3M holds the patent, but do you know the creator of Post-its, even though his story is often told to illustrate the creative thinking process?

Arthur Fry, a chemical engineer, invented Post-its. His creative process made a connection between the little pieces of paper which marked the songs to be sung in his church hymnal and a semi-sticky adhesive developed by Spencer Silver, another 3M researcher. Fry figured he could apply Silver's "temporarily-permanent" adhesive to his little pieces of paper, and he wouldn't have to worry about them dropping out of the hymnal. They would stick as long as he needed but would pull off without damaging the paper.

Fry represents a perfect example of an innovator who had the vision, commitment, and authority to own his idea enough, and then to own the idea enough to let go of it. He made the strange familiar by gaining the acceptance of those who could turn his idea into a reality, those who also had to own his idea. His way of selling his idea was almost as creative as the idea itself.

What's involved when it comes to getting others to buy into your idea? First, answer two fundamental questions:

- Who do you have to sell?
- How do you sell those people?

To begin with, make a list of people you need. In compiling this list, be sure to look at two constituent groups: those who can assist you, and those who might resist or block your idea. The two groups might be one in the same, but begin by making a list of those people who can assist you. They are people who have:

- Decision making and budgetary authority
- Expertise and skills you need
- The power to influence others
- Resources you need
- Something to gain from helping you

Those who might resist your idea feel they have more to lose than they have to gain, which reflects people's resistance to change. Whether it is time, money, or ego at risk, people need to understand clearly what they stand to lose if they don't change. Use this technique to change perception. This also requires creative thinking and creative selling.

Once you have listed all the people you need, prioritize the list by who can help you the most and at what step along the way. In Fry's case, when the idea first struck, 3M's Chairman of the Board might have had the most authority and the most power to influence others, but the chairman was not the first person on the list. Fry needed more than the concept. He needed a product. Who had the most expertise, skill, as well as something to gain? The R&D department and Spencer Silver. Fry approached them for a prototype.

With a prototype in hand Fry might have gone to the CEO or the chairman — but he didn't. He thought that if he had the marketing department behind him, it might be a cleaner sale to show the real authorities an opportunity they could not miss. Unfortunately, the marketing department was not interested.

This course of events lead Fry back to his list of "whos." Well, Fry decided to distribute sample Post-its to people who had the most power and opportunity to influence others: secretaries.

Secretaries, he figured, could demonstrate the use and, thus, the need for the product. He began with the chairman's secretary. Other secretaries began calling her, asking about the handy little notes. Soon, the requests became overwhelming. When the secretary called Fry for more, he directed her requests to the marketing department. And it didn't take many requests from the chairman's secretary for marketing to catch on. They changed their minds and suddenly became interested — very interested. The rest, as they say, is history. Marketing at 3M, by the way, took a lesson from Fry. When Post-its were finally introduced into the marketplace, they began by sending samples to the secretaries of the CEOs of all the Fortune 500 companies.

This example shows us just how critical it is to understand everyone who might help. Fry was not only creative in his invention, but he continued to tap that creativity to get his idea accepted. He considered all the obvious people, but he held off for a more effective and creative solution. It paid off handsomely for him and for the company.

HOW TO SELL YOUR IDEA

As Arthur Fry demonstrated, even good ideas require creative selling. We not only need to identify the people whose acceptance we need, we need to understand their perspective. Henry Ford said it well: "If there is any secret of success, it lies in the ability to get the other person's point of view and see things from his angle as well as from your own."

Just as we described the four faces of creativity in Chapter One as playing a major role in innovation, those same four faces represent the key to creative selling if we want to see our idea from another person's point of view.

there are four faces to creativity

The Analyzer, Implementor, Collaborator, and Imaginator in us buy for different reasons, sell through different approaches, and see the risks of change through different eyes. The degree to which our thinking style aligns with one of the four faces determines how much we utilize that style in making buying decisions or accepting new ideas. So different is each face in the way it thinks, processes, and receives information, it is as if they each speak a different language. Each style, then, demands a totally different way of communicating.

Obviously, communication flows fairly freely when your own thinking style is the same as the person you want to influence. If you are an Implementor and you are looking for support from another Implementor, just do what comes naturally.

The challenge arises in influencing a person whose preferred style is your least preferred style. "Lo siento mucho. No le comprendo." "Je suis desole. Je ne comprends pas." "I'm sorry. I don't understand."

Creative selling requires tapping your understanding of the skills and attributes of each of the four faces of creativity. While one of those faces may come naturally and easily, the others might require new skills.

Before you can begin learning the language of each style, it is important to become aware of your own unique thinking style and be able to identify the style of others. Having profiled the thinking styles of hundreds of our clients and client groups using the Herrmann Brain Dominance Survey[1] and the Choice Point Survey, each experience continues to validate the profound results encountered by people who discover their "most" and "least" preferred modes and the vast implications for growth. We have excerpted a portion of the Choice Point Survey, if you choose to try it for yourself in Appendix C.

Having scored your own survey and plotted your answers into each of the columns, you may have begun to sense the relationship of your responses to the style of thinking of each of the four faces. In fact, each ranking you made forms the pattern of your most and your least preferred mode, and if you recheck your choices you will begin to see clues which will help you identify others' styles as well.

Whether it is a planning or problem-solving situation on the job, how you select your leisure activities, what you prefer in your surroundings, or what you remember about the last book you read, you were influenced by your dominant thinking mode. The degree of difference between your highest and lowest scores illustrates the degree of dominance you have for that mode. Some people have two preferences and two least preferred styles and some are more balanced between all four. The explanations that follow will help you see the degree to which you and others are dominant in each of the four styles.

The Analyzer

THE ANALYZER THINKS SEQUENTIALLY AND LOGICALLY

---

[1] The Herrmann Brain Dominance Survey was authored by Ned Herrmann, a North Carolina-based consultant, educator, artist, and brain researcher. Ned inspired our interest and initiated our learning in a field he has pioneered. The rich foundation which Ned Herrmann provides in his teaching and sharing with colleagues gave birth to the Choice Point Survey, our metaphor of the four faces of creativity and the continued research and application we are pursuing in the field of "whole brain technologies."

Remember Walt from our discussion of the "Four Faces of Creativity" in Chapter One? Walt is the finance man who is good with numbers and doesn't drink wine without knowing its vintage. Some people might call him critical, although we prefer the term "discerning." Numbers and statistics mean a great deal to him, and precise measurement impresses him. When shopping for his new stereo, for example, he would not think of listening to speakers without first seeing their specs, and it took him months to make his final decision. Walt is an Analyzer.

Analyzers think sequentially and logically. They are intrigued with facts and credible (by their standards and logic) information. They are interested in quantity and numerical comparison. They are discerning in their tastes, love a good debate, enjoy questioning everything, and every answer they hear leads to a new question. If they aren't satisfied with the answer, they will make an objection. Furthermore, they are deliberate in coming to a decision. Analyzers are often numbers people which may lead them into careers as accountants, researchers, mathematicians, and computer technicians. They are more likely to prefer tangible than intangible results from your idea. The environment and conversation of an Analyzer reflects their valuing of efficiency and high performance. If something visual needs to be presented to an Analyzer, use pictures, specs, or mock-ups. Their decisions are based on logic — never intuition. The ideas they are most likely to accept will be those in which there is a measurable payoff.

Analyzers ask "what" and "how much" questions. They are interested in quantity. They want to know: "What are the facts?" "What are the features?" "How much does it cost?" "What does the research say?" "What resources are needed?" "What tests have been run?" "What analysis has been made?" "What justifies the risk?" "How much will it increase the bottom line?"

In presenting an idea to an Analyzer:

- Do your homework and never present an idea which has not been thoughtfully scrutinized, evaluated, analyzed, justified, and tested. Think of all the possible objections which may come up and have logical responses in your conscious awareness.

- Make an appointment ahead of time, telling the Analyzer how much time you need. Then be on time both arriving and leaving.

- Support the Analyzer's sequential, logical approach by being sequential and logical in your presentation.

- Provide a solid, factual foundation for the idea backed by solid research and data (financial and technical).

- Accompany your verbal presentation with a written presentation. You might want to include anticipated questions or objections with answers.

- If appropriate, present visual interpretations of the idea showing what it will look like. Analyzers have difficulty creating "mental pictures" from verbal descriptions.

- Since Analyzers are less able to imagine a visual representation, help them out by accompanying your presentation with graphs and charts if they will help validate the idea, or offer the Analyzer an opportunity to analyze the idea.

- If possible, give the Analyzer variations of the idea. They prefer making comparisons as part of the decision making process.

- Include a method to measure the results of implementing your idea. The Analyzer enjoys the opportunity for an ongoing audit.

- Never ask for an immediate decision. If you do, you will probably get a "no," since the Analyzer wants to weigh things before deciding. They like time to come up with more "whats" and potential objections. Do set a next meeting, though, since they will respect your sequential expectation. And make yourself available in between for answering any more questions that might come up.

If you are a Collaborator, the opposite of an Analyzer, don't feel intimidated or insulted by all the "what" questions and objections. The Analyzer is just doing what comes naturally. The questions and objections are not aimed at you or even your idea. Instead, they measure the logic of the risk the Analyzer must take in order to accept your idea and/or support it. If you yourself are a logical analyzer, during your presentation just make sure the two logics are the same.

The Implementor

Implementors are doers. They like structure and a system...

Kathleen was our Implementor from Chapter One. She is the meticulous list-keeper who is always punctual, well-organized, and who has her books and records indexed and alphabetized. Kathleen values procedure, order, and consistency. For her, neatness counts, and so do details. She is a true believer in the clean-desk policy, in fact, she probably instigated it, and she rarely leaves for home without meeting her goals for the day. Kathleen is an Implementor.

Implementors, like Analyzers, process information in a sequential manner, but they are doers more than thinkers. You will find Implementors in careers that involve hands-on activities such as manufacturing managers, the military, administrative assistants, and purchasing agents. They are organizers, methodical in their approach, giving great attention to detail. Implementor's environments reflect their traditional, safe-keeping values. They are more interested in the details of "how" than in the concept of a successful innovation. Like the Analyzer, they are unlikely to be visual or spacial, yet what they will most likely want to see will be an action plan, structure, or system, rather than a picture and a prototype — both of which are still important. They look for quality and reliability. Their decisions are based on practicality, predictability, usefulness, and precise methodology, not on hunches.

Implementors ask "how" questions. They want to know: "How will it be used?" "How does it work?" "How can we make money on it?" "How can we sell it?" "How will we implement it?" "How can we manufacture it?" "How can we be sure it will work?" "How do we know anyone will buy it?" With these questions, they are really saying is "Show me!"

In presenting an idea to an Implementor:

- Never surprise them. Prepare the Implementor ahead of presenting your idea by building a step-by-step approach which makes your idea seem like the next logical step of a useful progression. The idea should *enhance* rather than *revolutionize.*

- Don't *tell* them how it will be used. Show them, teach them, and let them try it. Remember, they are "hands on" people.

- Don't emphasize newness. Instead, emphasize how it combines pieces of tried and true experience, components, or methodologies.

- Either present implementation plans or engage the Implementor in assisting in that part of the process. It is what they like to do best.

- Highlight the procedural, practical problems your idea will solve along with the "how tos."

- Provide written details and instructions which can be followed in a 1-2-3 fashion.

- Make lists of questions or objections the Implementor raises and then respond to them sequentially and accurately. If you don't know the answer, be honest, but be sure to find out and then follow through by getting back in a timely manner. That is what an Implementor would do and so expects.

If you are the opposite of an Implementor, an Imaginator, do not feel put off or impatient with all of the "how" questions or objections. The Implementor phrases risk as "Is it do-able?" "Does it fit?" "Is it practical?" and "Is it appropriate?" If your idea says yes to these questions, you will get the support of the Implementor.

Though the Analyzer tends to think, and the Implementor tends to do, both represent the metaphorical example of left-brain, sequential, linear, logical processing. Both Analyzers and Implementors appreciate focused conversation which progresses step by step, and they generally find diversions distracting. They both prefer to receive their information in written form, and use it in formulating opinions and decisions. Your credibility and your success at gaining their acceptance rests on whether or not you can back up an organized presentation with facts and features.

The other two styles, the Imaginator and Collaborator, follow the metaphorical example of right-brain, simultaneous, synthesizing, intuitive processing. Their conversations roam since they are bored by staying on a focused track. Gaining their acceptance has more to do with pushing their emotional hot buttons or integrating your idea into their big picture. Benefits will speak louder than facts and features.

The Imaginator

Remember Sandy, the marketing manager who always has crazy ideas, and who is neither organized nor on time? She likes to keep a lot of balls up in the air at once. Her desk is a disaster, a blizzard of papers and files, all current projects. Some people find her frustrating to talk to because she never sticks to one topic. Sandy is an Imaginator.

The Imaginator thinks in a synthesizing, simultaneous manner. To Imaginators, one plus one equals three, not the logical two. One idea leads to another since their inner eye constantly sees random associations. These idea people are often found in jobs which have a creative thrust, whether in a planning or an artistic role. Their environments are visually stimulating, with an eclectic flair which might include both antiques and a Picasso print, side by side. Their desks will look busy (cluttered, according to an Analyzer or Implementor because desks are often a metaphor of our thinking style). They do not work in a sequential flow, they like to flit between projects, just as with topics of conversation, as the spirit moves them. Besides, they can find anything in those piles on their desks, and if they were ever to file something — well, out of sight, out of mind, perhaps never to be seen again.

In a problem-solving role, they are known to move on to new solutions before their last one was implemented. Newness is their middle name, and they are bored with details, preferring overall concepts.

Imaginators are more likely to be visionaries than tacticians, and intuition replaces logic when it comes to decision making. They like risk-taking ideas when they can visualize the big picture, but don't be surprised if they want to add their own ideas to yours.

Imaginators ask "if" questions. They want to know: "If this is a good idea, then what are the next possibilities?" "If there isn't a risk, then what is new?" "If it's been done before, how can we add a new twist?" When they ask "What if. . .," they are beginning to see and own the idea.

In presenting an idea to an Imaginator:

- While doing your homework, consider how your idea fits into the Imaginator's big picture. This means you must either see the big picture yourself or find it out.

- Identify the unique factors in your idea.

- Since Imaginators prefer spontaneity over schedules, you might arrange your meeting with them on the day you want to see them. If that doesn't work, don't feel rejected or unimportant if they reschedule or are not there when you arrive. It's nothing personal.

- Begin your meeting by inviting them to explore their vision and big picture.

- Spontaneity is also a necessity in the language and conversation. Try operating from a general outline. A sequential flow will only bore them, and you will find yourself frustrated and disorganized by their diversions.

- Don't bother with written presentations or proposals, since they probably won't read them, anyway.

- Emphasize concepts over details.

- Make your points through metaphor and analogy. They relate best to mental pictures.

- Invite them to add to your idea: it is the best way to get their buy-in.

- Ask them "If. . ." questions which ignite their imaginations.

- Don't down play the risk factor; in fact, you might play it up if it fits their big picture.

- Though they will not want to hear the details and implementation plans, they will want to know that someone will take care of them. Let them know they can depend on you for that.

In trying to gain an insight into an Imaginator's response to your idea, just ask them how they feel about it or ask if anything is missing. Their intuitive response will be important.

Finally, if you sense a positive feeling about your idea, get an immediate commitment. If you give them time to think about it, their imaginations will take over and you might not recognize your own idea when you get back to them for a decision.

If you are an Implementor, the opposite of an Imaginator, don't feel insulted when they change the subject, it is just imagination at work. Flow with their process. If you, too, are an Imaginator, remember that it is only your ideas or concepts that might clash. Go for trying a shared vision and a synthesis of your ideas. If your idea has a place in their holistic approach, if it has room for their imagination to play a role, and if it offers the excitement of risk and newness, you stand a good chance of gaining acceptance and support.

The Collaborator

Collaborators like gatherings

Bob the salesman is our Collaborator, the coach and confessor. He is constantly taking care of people's feelings, and empathizes strongly with others. He loves working in teams because he enjoys the dynamics of a group.

And his genuine concern for others inspires him to volunteer for a variety of causes. Bob is one of those people who is popular with just about everyone.

The Collaborator also thinks in a simultaneous rather than a linear style, but, like the Implementor, he is also more of a doer than a thinker. Their desks resemble the Imaginator's, if they have one. They are more likely to be out and about in their jobs. Collaborators are feeling people, and they have a good feeling for people. You will find them in people professions from selling to counseling. They take in information through their senses and integrate their experiences. They remember experiences which hold deep meaning to them. They aim to produce harmony from discord and turn ambiguity into shared purpose. They are sensitive to the emotions of others. Collaborators are empathizers, relating to human needs and looking for benefits in ideas rather than features, originality, or practicality. They revere interpersonal relationships, and their decisions often evolve from intuitive feelings about the needs they sense in people. You can usually find them championing a cause for the greater good.

Collaborators ask "why" questions. They want to know: "Why will people find satisfaction in this idea?" "Why will people buy it?" "Why will it produce a meaningful experience?" "Why do you like the idea?" "Why do you care?" "Why will they care?"

In presenting an idea to a Collaborator:

- Familiarize yourself with their key relationships, their causes, and their interests.

- When meeting with them, provide a climate inviting an interpersonal relationship — one that says you care about them and are interested in the people they care about.

- They usually enjoy a social setting, lunch or at least a cup of coffee. Tune into the Collaborator's mood and feelings.

- Be open and empathic.

- Integrate your idea into a concept which meets needs they recognize and identify. Present benefits they relate to.

- Give them an opportunity to get input from other people before making a decision. Let them know you will help them present the idea, though they are good at selling and might not need you.

- Since Collaborators like sharing experiences, give them the opportunity to be a part of a team approach in making a decision or implementing the idea.

All the facts in the world will not convince a Collaborator to accept your idea unless those facts are somehow related to personal benefits. It may be interesting to note that most sales professionals are Collaborators. They are naturally adept at tuning into other people, discovering their needs and, thus, matching those needs with the benefits of the product. In fact, the most professional salespeople say they do not sell products, they sell solutions to problems. When it comes to accepting an idea, Collaborators are most likely to accept one solving a human problem.

We have been looking at gaining acceptance through the thinking styles of the four faces of creativity. Each face is an integral part of us, even though one or two may be more natural or dominant. To access our full potential means "overcoming our own conditioning" and trying the language of each style, even the one we least prefer. That is possible, and it can be profitable.

We conduct a seminar entitled "Creative Communications" that includes learning to talk the language of each style, especially the least preferred. During a role play in one of our workshops, an advertising executive named Art jumped up and shouted, "Now, I've got it! I understand why I haven't been able to convince my client to buy into the promotional campaign I created for his firm. I see it! My client is an Analyzer, and I'm an Imaginator. I've been talking at him for a year, but I wasn't talking his language."

He left the workshop committed to trying a new approach — a new language. After ordering spec samples, putting together a written proposal dealing with each of the components of the proposal in a sequential flow, and making a formal presentation to the client, Art called to say he had walked out of his client's office with a large contract.

We also heard from Clarence, a newspaper controller and Analyzer whose least preferred style was the Collaborator. He had been trying, quite unsuccessfully, to work with the ad director, a Collaborator, to get ideas for reducing errors in ad transmittals, a billing document giving factual information about the advertiser and the ad. Finally, Clarence tried listening with a Collaborator's ears: he ended up trying the Collaborator's ideas, which included simplifying the form with symbols, graphics, and color codes instead of numbers. The form was accepted by the ad director and his reps, because it talked their language, not Clarence's. And it reduced errors by 80 percent.

Occasionally, we are asked if it isn't manipulative or deceitful to break your habitual mode of being when trying to influence another. Our response is yes — if in doing so you are a manipulative, deceitful person.

On the other hand, is it deceitful or manipulative to learn French when you expect to be living in Paris for a year? Or is it honoring the people you wish to communicate with? Americans are sometimes spoiled because other nationalities learn our language and we can often get by just being ourselves. But when we don't learn other languages, and the alternative perceptions they provide, then we are limiting ourselves.

Once we identify the style and language of the Analyzer, the Implementor, the Imaginator, and the Collaborator, we can use each of those four faces in communicating our desires and our ideas.

This is a good time to test your ability to identify the style and language of some of the people in your life — people you would like to influence.

Write down three people in each category: Analyzers, Implementors, Imaginators, and Collaborators.

Circle those who speak your least preferred language style. Sometimes we can learn from analyzing a past experience, so think of a time when you could not gain acceptance or influence one of these people. Write it down.

Write down how you presented your idea or concept.

Now, go back and read through the section describing the category in which that individual fits. Review the suggested presentation ideas as well. See if any of those suggestions were part of your presentation. Imagine that you have the opportunity to present your idea or concept again. What would you do differently? Write that down.

You might want to repeat this exercise with people who represent other styles and see if you gain any other personal insights on how you might achieve their acceptance.

Once you have analyzed some past experiences, you might want to concentrate on the present. Think of an idea you would like to implement. Write it down.

Now, list all the people whose acceptance you need. Beside each name, write their preferred thinking style.

Circle three people you need the most. Review the style of that person and the suggested presentation ideas. Now, let your imagination take over and mentally rehearse the process of presenting your idea, from making an appointment to hearing them say, "Great, you're on!"

Next, you might want to practice in front of the mirror. Anticipate the responses you will receive. If you really want to prepare and the stakes are high, we recommend a dress rehearsal.

Dress rehearsal is role-playing your presentation with a support person who has the same thinking style as the person you want to sell. If you cannot find that stand-in, ask someone to pretend. That may seem extreme, but if the idea is important, it could mean the difference between acceptance and rejection.

So far, we have been talking about communicating one-on-one to each specific style, as if we always had that option. One-to-one is the best place to start and to practice, but once you have mastered each style, you are ready to present an idea to a group.

Gaining Group Acceptance

A group of people will likely be a mixture of all four styles, whether the group is a department, an executive committee, or a task force. Group presentations, therefore, should address all four thinking styles.

This advice usually elicits questions such as:

"How can I be sequential and spontaneous all at the same time?"

"How can I bring in facts, details, and figures, without boring the Imaginators?"

"If I use metaphors and analogies, will I seem like a poet and turn off the Implementors?"

"Will the Analyzers see meaningful human benefits as emotional drivel?"

Well, as the saying goes, "You can't please all of the people all of the time, but you can please all of the people some of the time." One of the reasons some people have difficulty selling a group is that they do what comes naturally: they present from and to their preferred style. This sells some of the people all of the time — and the rest of the people none of the time. The key is to please all of the people some of the time.

THE IDEA IS MUSIC

Making a group presentation is like conducting a symphony orchestra, and the idea is the music. Just as a composition needs a group of musicians, each playing individual instruments in harmony to bring a standing ovation, so a business idea most often requires a group of people in order to be successfully implemented. For a moment, return to the notion of owning the idea enough to let go of it.

Before you begin presenting your idea to a group, you must be psychologically willing to share ownership of that idea with the group. In fact, finding new ownership is your real mission in making the presentation. With a standing ovation as a metaphorical vision of your idea being implemented, you might ask yourself, "As the symphony conductor, what will I have to accomplish with these musicians to realize my vision?"

Take a minute to imagine all of the implications this metaphor suggests for making group presentations. Below are a few components which may provide you with seeds for associations while previewing your role. If you can think of others, add them.

The Baton	Skills
Strings	The Performance
Brass	Applause
Woodwinds	Audience
Bass Drum	Rewards
Soloists	Sounds
Rhythm	Score
Rehearsals	Discord
Tuxedos	Themes
Schedules	Others

If you completed that exercise, you have begun the first step of making a presentation. You have used divergent, imaginative, metaphorical thinking to consider a multitude of components which can be organized into a plan for making a presentation. The exercise suggests ideas for two phases of making a presentation: preparation and presenting.

Preparation

There are many steps to the preparation for your presentation. The first step is to sit back and do the following serious thinking. Begin your preparation with the following three steps:

1. Divergent Thinking

Get into the style of the Analyzer, the Implementor, the Imaginator, and the Collaborator. Make lists which answer the "what," "how," "why," and "if" questions suggested previously. Do not skip this step, it forms the foundation for your presentation. Without it, you would be like a conductor without a score, which shows the music for each instrumental section.

2. Consider All Four Faces

With the previous list as a resource, answer the following questions (the answers become the major buy-in motive for each of the styles of people in the group):

- FOR THE ANALYZERS: What is the measurable payoff in my idea that makes the risk a logical decision?

- FOR THE IMPLEMENTORS: What is the practical, useful component of my idea that makes it a logical, do-able next step?

- FOR THE IMAGINATORS: What is the unique factor of my idea that fits the overall mission or shared vision?

- FOR THE COLLABORATORS: What problem can be solved or what human needs can be met by my idea?

3. Develop Your Strategy

Think of the paradoxical needs and styles within your group as the different instrumental groups within the orchestra. As the conductor, you understand the diversity of your tasks, and you know each member makes a unique contribution. The lonely percussionist in the rear is just as important as the large string section in the front. Your strategy is like scheduling and conducting the rehearsals in which you prepare, organize, coordinate, mentor, and inspire each musician to play with total dedication. You know all of their music, you know you need each of them, you know their individual risks, and now you must plan how to get their commitment as individuals, sub-groups, and as an inter-dependent whole.

Although you cannot reach all of your group all of the time, you can reach all of them some of the time. In looking at the overall presentation, shift your focus from the Imaginators, to the Analyzers, to the Implementors, and to the Collaborators in cycles and in a deliberate rhythm and with a sincere appreciation of their unique needs.

Scheduling

Timing is important. In your preparation process, be ready to give at least one week's notice for the sake of the Analyzers and Implementors respect of scheduling, but not more than two weeks for the Imaginators and Collaborators. Give Imaginators and Collaborators too much time, and they are sure to forget. Mondays are not good days because you compete with the mail and the weekly organizing of Analyzers and Implementors. Imaginators and Collaborators might not check their calendars and forget a Monday morning appointment. Fridays are not the best either since Analyzers and Implementors are into finishing up their week's tasks, and Collaborators and Imaginators are already thinking about the weekend. The same holds true on the day before a holiday. All of these are fairly gross generalizations; however, if you have the freedom to schedule the meeting, you might keep these considerations in mind.

We favor morning meetings for alertness but never before 9:30, since many Imaginators and Collaborators are night people and do not get going before then. By that time, the early risers are ready for a coffee break. Not only plan when your meeting will begin, but also when it will end. It should not go over an hour and a half, or you will lose their attention.

Meeting Logistics

Arrange for a conference room and coffee. In these health conscious days, it is also good to have juice and herbal tea as alternatives. Make refreshments available fifteen minutes before the meeting to allow Collaborators to socialize.

If possible, use a round conference table. The power seats of rectangular tables are at either end. If you sit at one end, those with the strongest objections are likely to sit at the other end. If you *must* operate with an oblong or rectangular table, however, plan to make your presentation from the middle of the longest side. Your objector will tend to sit at one of the power seats facing another objector, not you.

Since smokers are now minorities, why have smoke competing with your idea? Most smokers can last an hour and a half, but if there are complaints, take a smoking break in the middle and make everybody happy.

Resources

Plan and arrange for the resources which will best support your presentation. The following is a check list. Some of the items are optional, but most are essential.

☐ BLANK PAPER AND PENCILS. Analyzers and Implementors take meticulous notes. Imaginators and Collaborators like to doodle.

☐ THE CONTENT OF YOUR PRESENTATION. Provide a copy of your presentation for each person in the group. It should be in outline form and double-spaced, with room for notes. It should include visuals, graphics, charts, etc. to help clarify the whats, whys, hows, and ifs of the idea. This is a must for Analyzers and Implementors, and it provides more doodle space for Imaginators and Collaborators.

☐   AN OVERHEAD PROJECTOR AND TRANSPARENCIES. Summarize your content on overhead transparencies. With half-inch letters for easy reading, make no more than five points per transparency. If you have access to a computer and printer which can print in large letters, make originals on the computer, and copy them onto the transparencies with any photocopy machine. You may also use felt pens for your transparencies.

The Imaginators would love it if you spiced them up with various colors. The Analyzers and Implementors will appreciate following your sequence, and they will feel you are prepared and credible. If you are an Imaginator or Collaborator, the transparencies will keep you on track, while at the same time allowing you to talk off the cuff.

☐   A FLIP CHART. If you cannot make transparencies, put the same information on a flip chart for the same reasons. Even if you have transparencies, you will need the flip chart to write objections which can be followed by writing your response.

☐   A DRAWING OR PROTOTYPE. This is important if your idea is a product.

☐   PEOPLE. Sometimes, it is valuable to have other people involved, especially technological experts if necessary. If they can not be physically at the meeting, include their testimony or written explanations.

☐   DEMONSTRATION MATERIALS. Some ideas require a demonstration. If your idea is one of these, prepare for it as part of your strategy.

☐   RESEARCH REPORTS. If you have already piloted your idea, include a full report on the results.

Order Your Content

Set up expectations.

In Section Two, you answered four questions. Begin your presentation with the answers to these questions in the following order:

- The problem your idea solves (for the Collaborator in each person).

- The measurable payoff which makes the risk a logical decision (for the Analyzer in each person).

- The practical, useful component of your idea which makes it a logical, do-able next step (for the Implementor in each person).

- The unique factor that fits an overall mission or shared vision (for the Imaginator in each person).

By addressing these issues up front, you tell the group why they should listen to you and pique their interest.

- Show them the idea.

- Answer the four basic questions.

In Section One, you developed a list of whys, whats, hows, and ifs. Select the most appropriate answer to each question and give them to the group in the above order.

- Counter potential objections.

If you anticipate many objections, you may want to counter them at this point, before someone else raises them. Organize your list as follows:

Questions   Answers

_____   _____

_____   _____

- Summarize, and challenge commitment.

Return to the expectations you set above. Re-word your answers if you like, but make sure they say the same thing. Challenge them to take the risk and make the commitment.

Optional Strategy for Gaining Commitment

Once you have moved through the content of your presentation, be prepared for two possibilities:

1. If they are ready to give you a positive commitment, then ask for it.
2. If you feel they need time to make a decision, then be prepared for the next step — another meeting. This may require additional homework on their part or yours. Be prepared to tell them what you both will have to do, and by when.

Rehearse

Just as with individual one-on-one presentations, envision your whole presentation one step at a time. Then do it in front of a mirror. Finally, practice on a support group, perhaps your family.

Presentation

Invitation

The presentation starts with a memo, a letter, or phone call to invite their involvement. Give them a hint of the rewards they can expect. This is the beginning of setting expectations. Let them know you need them and why. Announce the time you will serve refreshments, and when the meeting will begin and end. Do not forget the location, nor others who will be present at the meeting.

Make Presentation

Having developed your strategy, prepared your resources, and practiced your presentation — relax. Stick to your plan and have fun. Have a sense of humor, don't take yourself too seriously. If you make a mistake, remember that you have resources backing you up. Enjoy these people, and think about how happy they will be when your shared idea, your composition, receives a standing ovation.

Ask for Commitment

Sales professionals call this step "asking for the order." When push comes to shove, many of us buckle when it comes to the moment of facing a yes or no. Some people just never get around to asking for the order. To avoid rejection, others oversell, boring their customers until they change their mind. Don't make that mistake. Use your Imaginator's intuition or your Analyzer's logic to know when you have acceptance, and then hoist your baton and begin the symphony of agreement. Your idea will become a reality.

SUMMARY

The implementation of an idea depends on gaining acceptance at many steps along the way. It is difficult, if not impossible, to separate the selling of ideas from implementing them. The process demands sensitivity to yourself, as well as to others. It demands attention to detail and process, in addition to a thorough analytical understanding of the idea and its political and financial environment. Implementation also demands imagination and intuition.

Selling an idea requires you to tap all four faces of creativity to be certain it is understood. No one wins by overlooking the potential of a good idea.

The responsibility to sell the idea is yours. You, alone, fully understand its potential. Effective selling assures that good ideas are implemented by your company, not by the competition.

Fool Proof
Implementation

Defeating Murphy's Law

Creativity is more than imagination, it is imagination inseparably coupled with both intent and effort.

— Alex Osborne

Throughout the book, we have discussed the importance of ideas and how they can lead to a rewarding and successful business life. But in another sense, ideas are a dime a dozen. Unless you can implement them, develop a course of action, and make it happen, you are actually worse off than when you only had the problem. Once you have an idea, the gap between what could be and what is is more real and tangible, and you know something could be done to solve it.

Although with viable ideas to solve your problem your world is now full of opportunities, you also bear the responsibility of those opportunities, both to yourself and to your business. This can be difficult. The challenge is to be as creative about the way you make your ideas a reality as you have been in developing them. Accept the challenge, and your chances of success are high.

Many people have ideas, but few are truly creative. Unless ideas are realized, they remain ephemeral. When they become implemented in some way, they become creations — and those who transform ideas into creations are creative.

Implementation poses such difficulty because everything and everybody involved in your scheme has a deeply rooted interest in resisting. Change, even positive change, causes stress. It is a simple law of physics. Things and people need to be stopped, started, prodded, sold, bought, rearranged, motivated, re-tooled, revamped, and recharged. The energy to overcome an inertial world flows from your perseverance and your vision of the possibilities.

This chapter presents a step-by-step implementation plan for solutions requiring creative change. It continues with the example begun in Chapter Three and looks at the steps involved in getting commitment and support from key individuals and in actually implementing the solutions. These steps insure your chances of success and put yourself, your colleagues, and your business into the best of all potential futures — the one you create yourself.

IMPLEMENTATION PLAN

1. Mental Events Slide Show
2. Activities List
3. Activities Review
4. Problem Activities
5. Selling the Idea
6. Developing Risk Insurance
7. Maximizing Gain
8. Attitude Checking
9. Taking the First Step

IMPLEMENTATION PLAN — **MENTAL EVENTS SLIDE SHOW**

→ 1 MENTAL EVENTS SLIDE SHOW
2. Activities List
3. Activities Review
4. Problem Activities
5. Selling the Idea
6. Developing Risk Insurance
7. Maximizing Gain
8. Attitude Checking
9. Taking the First Step

There is nothing so sublime as sitting quietly and sipping a cup of tea in full knowledge of events that have not yet taken place.

— Wu Fat (Arch Villain), *Hawaii 5-0*

Think about a typical slide show and how, with a series of snapshots, it tells a story in images. Each slide presents the next event in a progression which leads the viewer from beginning to end.

The Mental Events Slide Show creates the same kind of progression, beginning with a solution and ending with the actual implementation of an idea. The snapshots which document the steps to implementation, however, appear only in the mind — the ultimate in instant photography.

THE SAGA CONTINUES

To illustrate this process, we continue where we left off in Chapter Three, with the PCP example.

When last we saw our characters, they had decided on a solution — to assign key scientists from the R&D lab temporarily to the plant, allowing them to work directly with the commercial machines and plant personnel to discover and solve the problems plaguing the production of the diaper facing material.

Although those involved in the creative session felt sure that this solution, in concept, would lead to both short- and long-term fixes for the problem, they feared potential opposition from a variety of people, for a variety of reasons.

As we proceed through the example, notice how implementation considers the thinking styles of the executives and managers involved, and takes their styles into account in the planning and implementation process.

As we mentioned in previous chapters, it is most important to follow the *process* we use; the example simply illustrates the kinds of thinking we are suggesting for implementing your own solutions to your own problems.

The PCP organization chart appears below and may be helpful as you proceed.

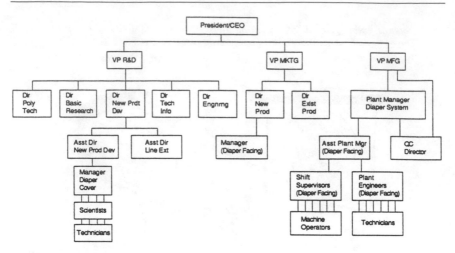

A. Fill-In Key Column

Using a Forced Relationship Form, title the Key Column "Implementation Events." Take a minute to sit back and calm your thoughts. After you have relaxed, imagine that the implementation of your solution is actually happening. Try to see people, machines, events that are behaving, working, and occurring exactly the way you want them to. See yourself in this scene. Look around. What is happening? Indulge your imagination. Finally, after creating a clear picture of what you want to have happen as a result of your solution, write one or two brief sentences describing what you see.

> Note that the responses which follow are from the point of view of the Research Manager.

PCP EXAMPLE

(Key Column) Implementation Events	(Insight Column)
1. R&D and plant people are working together at the plant site instituting quick fixes as well as developing a long term understanding of the commercialization process. They are led by a mgmt team of the Asst. Research Director and the Asst. Plant Manager.	

B. Prior Event

Assuming that what we just imagined comes true, think about the events that would have to happen immediately prior to this final scenario. What logical step would have to occur to make the final scenario happen? Again, assume that things happen exactly as you want them to. If it helps, close your eyes, think about the people or equipment involved and "watch" them doing exactly what you want. Record this scenario next.

PCP EXAMPLE

(Key Column) Implementation Events	(Insight Column)
1. R&D and plant people are working together at the plant site instituting quick fixes as well as developing a long term understanding of the commercialization process. They are led by a mgmt team of the Asst. Research Director and the Asst. Plant Manager. 2. A team-building session has been held with all the players at the plant site to develop a new vision and define roles and responsibilities. The meeting is chaired by the Asst. Director of New Product Development and by the Asst. Plant Manager.	

C. Work Backwards In Time

Repeat Step B, working backwards one step at a time. Each entry describes the event immediately preceding it. Continue this process until reaching your situation as it exists today.

PCP EXAMPLE

(Key Column)	(Insight Column) Implementation Events
1. R&D and plant people are working together at the plant site instituting quick fixes as well as developing a long term understanding of the commercialization process. They are led by a mgmt team of the Asst. Research Director and the Asst. Plant Manager. 2. A team-building session has been held with all the players at the plant site to develop a new vision, and define roles and responsibilities. The meeting is chaired by the Asst. Director of New Product Development and by the Asst. Plant Manager. 3. The Asst. Director of New Product Development and a portion of the R&D dept. has just temporarily relocated to plant site and have taken over a portion of the plant QC lab. Concurrently, some of the plant engineers have temporarily transferred to R&D where they are reporting directly to the Director of New Product Development.	

Slide Show examples four through eight can be found in Appendix E.

PCP EXAMPLE

(Key Column)	(Insight Column) Implementation Events
9. The Research Mgr. of diaper facing meets with his boss, the Asst. Director of New Product Development, to present the R&D solution and ask for help in the implementation. 10. (Present) The creative session has ended. The research manager's solution is to create an ad hoc team of research scientists and plant engineers which will be lead by a joint, two-person team consisting of the Asst. Director of New Product Dev. and the Asst. Plant Manager for diaper facing. The operation's responsibility will fall to the Research Manager who will have both the R&D scientists and a portion of the plant engineers reporting directly to him. He, in turn, reports periodically in problem solving meetings to the two-person committee. The operation is located in the QC portion of the plant. Meanwhile, a small group of plant engineers will be temporarily transferred to the R&D facility to report to the Director of New Product Dev. They are to learn about emerging technologies, and fill the void created by the scientists who left for the plant. The whole issue must be resolved, and the plant operations must show significant improvement in six months.	

Reading now backwards, you have developed your initial implementation scheme. Check and see if there might be intermediate stages you have omitted. If so, insert them before proceeding.

In working with your own problem, it is possible, depending on the complexity of your solution, that your list of implementation activities will be more involved than our example. We have shortened the process to show a variety of entries.

IMPLEMENTATION PLAN — **ACTIVITIES LIST**

	1.	Mental Events Slide Show
→	**2.**	**ACTIVITIES LIST**
	3.	Activities Review
	4.	Problem Activities
	5.	Selling the Idea
	6.	Developing Risk Insurance
	7.	Maximizing Gain
	8.	Attitude Checking
	9.	Taking the First Step

A. Assigning Dates

1. On the top left, next to your final scenario, record the date on which you expect (or need) this final phase to be working. This is your target implementation deadline.

2. Record today's date next to the bottom entry (the present).

3. Now, from this bottom entry, look at the very next event (in the left column). On the right, in the Insight Column beside that next event, record all the necessary activities for your next event to occur successfully.

Suggestions for activities include (but are not limited to) gaining available technology; getting people to buy-in; securing material, finances, or services; political and legal considerations; and dealing with formal policies and procedures.

4. Include the amount of time it will reasonably take to accomplish these activities.

5. Record the new date of implementation for the next Slide Show Event on the left by adding the appropriate number of days to the previous Slide Show Event date. In other words, estimate how much time is needed for the first step, add that time to today, and enter it in the step above the present state.

> In the following PCP example, the present date is 3/1 (found beside Event 10). In filling out this form, the Research Manager listed two activities necessary to complete Event 9. He estimated those activities would take one week. Adding seven days to the 3/1 date, he estimates completion of Event 9 on 3/8. He listed that estimated date next to the number nine on the Event side of the form. He then continued that process through the rest of the events.

PCP EXAMPLE

(Key Column) Implementation Events	(Insight Column) Activities for Next Step
10. (Present - 3/1) The creative session has ended. The research manager's solution is to create an ad hoc team of research scientists and plant engineers which will be lead by a joint, two-person team consisting of the Asst. Director of New Product Dev. and the Asst. Plant Manager for diaper facing. The operation's responsibility will fall to the Research Manager who will have both the R&D scientists and a portion of the plant engineers reporting directly to him. He, in turn, reports periodically in problem-solving meetings to the two-person committee.	

PCP EXAMPLE (CONTINUED)

(Key Column) Implementation Events	(Insight Column) Activities for Next Step
The operation is located in the QC portion of the plant. Meanwhile a small group of plant engineers will be temporarily transferred to the R&D facility to report to the Director of New Product Dev. They are to learn about emerging technologies, and fill the void created by the scientists who left for the plant. The whole issue must be resolved, and the plant operations must show significant improvement in six months. 9. (3/8) The Research Mgr. of diaper facing meets with his boss, the Asst. Director of New Product Development to present the R&D solution and ask for help in the implementation.	A. A marketing strategy document stating the solution, the necessary human and technical resources to make it work, and a rationale showing the proposal as the only reasonable hope of solving the problem in the six-month time frame. B. Convince him to relocate temporarily to the plant. (Time for completion: 1 week)

B. Continue Working Forward In Time

Working from the present to the future, repeat Step A, listing activities in the Insight Column for each entry in your implementation activities, adding the time necessary for the activities to the previous event to find the estimated completion date for the current event.

In developing your to-do list of activities, keep thinking about all that has to happen to make the next event occur.

PCP EXAMPLE

(Key Column) Implementation Events	(Insight Column) Activities for Next Step
8. (3/8) The Research Mgr. of diaper facing meets with the Research Asst. Dir. of New Product Development, Marketing Mgr. of diaper facing, and Asst. Plant Mgr. for diaper facing to present his proposal.	A. Availability of Asst. Plant Mgr., Asst. Dir. of NPD, and Mktg. Mgr. all in the same place at the same time. B. Buy-in from Assistant Plant Mgr. (Completion time: 1 week)

The full PCP example can be found in Appendix E.

PCP EXAMPLE (CONTINUED)

(Key Column) Implementation Events	(Insight Column) Activities for Next Step
2. (5/19) A team-building session has been held with all the players at the plant to develop a new vision, and to discuss roles and responsibilities. The meeting is chaired by the Asst. Director of New Product Development and by the Asst. Plant Manager.	A. Format worked out for joint task team meeting. B. Facilitators appointed and schooled in shared creative problem solving techniques. C. Developing new esprit in joint team. D. New roles and responsibilities agreed to by all participants. (Completion time: 3½ months)
1. (9/1) R&D and plant people are working together at the plant instituting quick fixes as well as developing a long term understanding of the commercialization process. They are led by a mgmt. team of the Asst. Research Director, and the Asst. Plant Manager.	A. Commercial process analyzed for short-term fixes. B. Long-term understanding work completed. C. All workers working with facing participating in quality and productivity problem solving sessions. D. Commercial quantities of on-spec goods produced for the market. (Completion time: 3½ months)

C. Checking Dates

Once you have worked through all the events, you should have two dates at the end: your target deadline date and the time it will take for you to accomplish your to-do list of activities. This is the first check on whether you will be able to implement your solution.

If you can complete your activities at the same time or sooner than your target deadline, you are in good shape. If your activities extend beyond your deadline, then you have your first creative challenge in the implementation plan. This problem is considered in the next step of the process.

IMPLEMENTATION PLAN — **ACTIVITIES REVIEW**

    1.   Mental Events Slide Show
    2.   Activities List
→   **3.   ACTIVITIES REVIEW**
    4.   Problem Activities
    5.   Selling the Idea
    6.   Developing Risk Insurance
    7.   Maximizing Gain
    8.   Attitude Checking
    9.   Taking the First Step

So far, you have used the Mental Events Slide Show to list the significant events which have to occur to implement your solution. In the Activities List, you created a to-do list of activities which need to be accomplished before moving on to the next event in the slide show.

Now it is time to review and evaluate each of the activities. Some of them can be accomplished easily, others can be accomplished with a reasonable amount of work. But it is natural for a few of the activities to present critical problems in the implementation process. The Activities Review helps you consider the relative difficulty of each activity on your list.

A. Create Activities Review Form

Develop a new three column sheet entitled "Activities Review." Label the left column ACTIVITY, the middle column RATING, and the right column RATIONALE. Leave room over the columns to write in the Slide Show Event. (See the following example.)

SLIDE SHOW EVENT

ACTIVITY *RATING* *RATIONALE*

B. Completing Activities Review Form

Working from the present into the future, pick the first implementation event from your Mental Events Slide Show which needs to occur. Write a short version of that event opposite the heading: SLIDE SHOW EVENT.

In the PCP example, the first event is number nine. (Event 10 is the present situation.)

9. (3/8) The Research Mgr. of diaper facing meets with his boss, the Asst. Director of New Product Development, to present the R&D solution and to ask for help in the implementation.

SLIDE SHOW EVENT   #9. Meeting with the Asst. Director of New Product Development.

ACTIVITY *RATING* *RATIONALE*

Then list in the Activity column all the activities which have to occur to bring that event about. (This information comes from the Activities List you completed in the previous step.)

> In the PCP example, the activities were described as follows:
>
> 1. Writing a marketing strategy document stating the solution, the necessary human and technical resources to make it work, and a rationale showing the proposal as the only reasonable hope of solving the problem in the six-month time frame.
> 2. Convince him (Asst. Dir. of New Product Development) to relocate temporarily to the plant.
>
> (See PCP example below.)

SLIDE SHOW EVENT   #9. Meeting with the Asst. Director of New Product Development.

ACTIVITY	RATING	RATIONALE
1. Marketing strategy document.		
2. Convince him to relocate temporarily to the plant.		

In the second column, evaluate the difficulty of each activity and assign it a value from one to three. In this system, a three is the easiest — a piece of cake, a rating of two can be done with effort, and a score of one is a problem activity needing further work.

> In the PCP example, they rated the marketing strategy document a three, and the job of convincing the Asst. Director of New Product Marketing to relocate temporarily to the plant, a one. (See example below.)

SLIDE SHOW EVENT   #9. Meeting with the Asst. Director of New Product Development.

ACTIVITY	RATING	RATIONALE
1. Marketing strategy document.	3	
2. Convince him to relocate temporarily to the plant.	1	

In the RATIONALE column, give reasons for the ratings you assigned each activity. Where you have a rating of one, record the major blocks or impediments causing the problem.

PCP listed the following rationale:

It's easy to show how the R&D solution is the only thing compatible with the marketing strategy.

It will be difficult to get him to agree to relocate.

(See example below.)

SLIDE SHOW EVENT

#9. Meeting with the Asst. Director of New Product Development.

	ACTIVITY	RATING	RATIONALE
1.	Marketing strategy document.	3	It's easy to show how the R&D solution is the only thing compatible with marketing strategy.
2.	Convincing him to relocate temporarily to the plant.	1	It will be difficult to get him to agree to relocate.

Continue the same process for each of your Slide Show Events, counting down to the final implementation.

In the PCP example, Event 8 is:

The Research Manager of diaper facing meets with the Research Assistant Director of New Product Development, the Marketing Manager of diaper facing, and the Assistant Plant Manager for diaper facing to present his proposal.

The entire example is listed below.

SLIDE SHOW EVENT

#8. Marketing meeting with the VP of Marketing.

	ACTIVITY	RATING	RATIONALE
1.	Availability of marketing funds to cover relocation costs	2	Within budget limits. Show how solution is cost effective.
2.	Buy-in by V.P. of Marketing	2	Feather in his cap to show how he can catalyze the interdisciplinary team. Shows his ability to take over for the CEO when he retires.

The entire PCP example of the Activities Review can be found in Appendix E.

After using this process for each of your Slide Show Events, review all your ratings and explanations. If you have no failing grades, skip the next section (Problem Activities) and go on to "Selling the Idea" (page 118). If timing is a problem, or if you have one or more failing grades, proceed to the next step.

IMPLEMENTATION PLAN — **PROBLEM ACTIVITIES**

> 1. Mental Events Slide Show
> 2. Activities List
> 3. Activities Review
→ 4. **PROBLEM ACTIVITIES**
> 5. Selling the Idea
> 6. Developing Risk Insurance
> 7. Maximizing Gain
> 8. Attitude Checking
> 9. Taking the First Step

In the previous section, we reviewed each of the activities necessary to make the Mental Slide Show happen. Some of those activities were relatively easy, some could be done with work, and others presented problems. If you have activities which pose problems for you, this section will help you with techniques for dealing with these problems.

A. Write Event, Activity, and Rationale

On a separate piece of paper, write down the Slide Show Event, the particular activity which rated a failing grade (one) in the Activities Review, and the Rationale for that activity which should list the major blockage for that particular activity. (See example below.)

SLIDE SHOW EVENT	#9. Meeting between the Research Manager and the Assistant Director of New Product Development.

ACTIVITY

Proposal and rationale acceptance by the Assistant Director of R&D and Director of New Product Development.

RATIONALE (OBSTACLE)

It will be difficult to get the Director of New Product Development to agree to relocate.

B. How to. . . Statements

Develop a list of "How to. . ." statements addressing ways to raise the rating to passing (two). Using Divergent Thinking, see how many opportunities you can develop using the words "How to. . ." to remove this blockage.

> In the following PCP example, notice how the "How to. . ." statement is used in a variety of ways to generate new ideas for solving the problem.

HOW TOs. . .

    How to get buy-in from the Assistant Director of New Product Development

    How to get him to see the personal benefit

    How to coerce him into accepting the job

    How to flatter him into accepting the job

✓   How to show him how this might help him get ahead in his career

The "How to. . ." statement is a powerful problem solving tool all by itself. Generating a variety of statements reveals many different options for producing problem solving ideas.

Notice that one specific technique used in the above example is to change the verb in the "How to. . ." statement.

C. Develop Ideas

Pick the one "How to. . ." statement which you feel has a chance of success. (If there are none, generate more "How tos. . .") Using Divergent Thinking, letting the Kid free, develop ideas for solving the problem.

✓   How to show him how this might help him get ahead in his career

> PCP has chosen this as the most likely to succeed with the Assistant Director of New Product Development.

IDEAS (For showing how this might help his career.)

    Show him how he will be largely responsible for success.

    Show him how the new task will broaden his skills.

    Show him how the V.P. of R&D will leverage this project into a promotion for him.

✓   Get the Marketing Manager for diaper facing to talk with him.

✓   Show him that he is the only one who can pull it off.

D. Dissect The Best Idea(s)

Pick the best idea or ideas and divide them into what is useful and what is missing. Dissecting Ideas is one of the four fundamental creative skills discussed in Chapter Two.

> Notice in the PCP example that they chose to combine two ideas into one.

✓   Get the Marketing Manager for diaper facing to talk with him.

✓   Show him that he is the only one who can pull it off.

WHAT'S USEFUL (about having the Marketing Manager talk to him and show him that he's the only one who can do the job?)

> The Marketing Manager has his ear.
>
> It creates a power position for him, and makes him a high profile person.
>
> He will be recognized by the V.P. of Marketing.

WHAT'S MISSING?

> How to get the Marketing Manager to talk with him?

E. Develop New Ideas for What's Missing

Reiterate the same idea generating process for filling in what is missing in the idea. If you have an idea that solves the problem completely, then move on to the next problem activity.

PCP felt their idea for filling in what was missing in the idea adequately solved this particular problem activity. They recognize that they could simply ask. He will be anxious to help and show his influence.

If you find yourself doing several iterations of generating ideas, choosing one or combining more than one, and dissecting them without coming to a satisfactory conclusion, you may need to go on to Chapter Six. Use one of the techniques outlined to develop new and potentially beneficial ideas to change your evaluation of the activity to a two or better.

Finally, if this fails, try developing ideas for circumventing or changing this particular event entirely. Look at what the event accomplishes, and explore different ways for accomplishing the same thing. For example, imagine that you need to buy a piece of machinery to develop a prototype, but the price is totally prohibitive. You might consider how to develop the prototype without machinery, how to do it by hand, how to use existing machinery, etc.

F. Continue For All Problem Activities

If you are working on your own problem, use this process to change all your problem activities from a score of one to a two or three.

Examples of how this technique was applied to other PCP problem activities can be found in Appendix E.

By this point, the patterns should be well established in your mind. Problems, How tos. . ., Ideas, What's Useful?, What's Missing? — and so on. This simple structure holds enormous power for dealing with almost any situation. You have seen it over and over in this book.

Combining this process with overcoming your implementation obstacles simply continues the creative process, a process that never really stops. Creative thinking is *always* useful, and when practiced, becomes a way of life.

IMPLEMENTATION PLAN — **SELLING THE IDEA**

1.	Mental Events Slide Show
2.	Activities List
3.	Activities Review
4.	Problem Activities
→ 5.	**SELLING THE IDEA**
6.	Developing Risk Insurance
7.	Maximizing Gain
8.	Attitude Checking
9.	Taking the First Step

So far, you have created a partial implementation plan which includes a series of critical events leading up to the moment of actual implementation, a list of activities to bring those events about, and bridges over (or around) the potential roadblocks in those activities.

All this detail work should have given you a clear idea of who the major players are going to be in your implementation. These are people whose cooperation, agreement, and support will be necessary to bring the implementation about.

Take a moment to think about how you are going to sell these people on their role in your implementation plan. After you have considered it, write a brief paragraph for each key player, describing their thinking styles (Analyzer, Implementor, Collaborator, or Imaginator) and those things about their behavior which indicate that style to you. Finally, indicate how presentations might best be focused for them.

If you need help remembering the characteristics of each style and how best to sell them, refer back to Chapter Four.

> The PCP example below focuses on the Vice President of Marketing and the Assistant Director of New Product Development. Other key players are discussed in Appendix E.

A. V.P. Of Marketing

He always talks about "the big picture." He dresses flamboyantly, and his office has several pieces of art in it. He gets bored very easily in meetings once he understands the agenda's major thrust. He endlessly doodles crazy geometric designs on a scratch pad. He is definitely an Imaginator. Present ideas to him by showing the overall concept with an attached flow diagram briefly outlining the significant events. Then point out why this solution is *different* from anything PCP has ever attempted in the past.

B. Assistant Director Of New Product Development

He searches for facts and figures. Driven by "quantity," he always seeks to compare results and hypotheses to other published results. He prides himself on being a "gatekeeper" and his ability to ask probing questions about the efficacy of any approach. He is an Analyzer. Approach him armed with huge amounts of data about machine performance, comparing situations where R&D is present and absent from the mill. Show him that he is the only one "smart enough" to be able to oversee the technical approaches that are being pursued.

IMPLEMENTATION PLAN — **DEVELOPING RISK INSURANCE**

	1.	Mental Events Slide Show
	2.	Activities List
	3.	Activities Review
	4.	Problem Activities
	5.	Selling the Idea
→	6.	**DEVELOPING RISK INSURANCE**
	7.	Maximizing Gain
	8.	Attitude Checking
	9.	Taking the First Step

In the most carefully controlled scientific experiments, the animals will do what they damn well please!

— Anonymous

We are all a little too familiar with Mr. Murphy's laws about the probabilities for things screwing up. They do. They will. And no one escapes it. So the best we can do is be prepared for it. In fact, we should plan for it and use our creative skills to help us foresee what might go wrong. Of course, we can not consider every eventuality, but by being clever and careful about how we proceed, we can eliminate some of the difficulties, or even better, turn them into positive consequences for ourselves.

We have no control over many of the upcoming events in our lives, but we have ultimate control over how we interact with them, and how we use them to our advantage.

This section outlines a brief technique for minimizing downside risk. It was first developed by Walt Disney in the late 1920's under the name of "Objection Countering," and a modification follows.

A. Cast A Group

Find a group of two or three people who share these characteristics:

1. They have fertile, fluent minds and have no problem voicing their opinions.
2. They are Analyzers. Consider financial types, lawyers, engineers, plant operations, and manufacturing types.
3. They have at least a nodding acquaintance with your situation but are not so embroiled in it that they cannot be objective. (You might consider people with whom you have had some past difficulty. This shows them how much you value their input.)

> For this meeting, PCP brought together the Assistant Director for Line Extension, the Director of Basic Research, and the Plant Quality Control Director.
>
> Both the Assistant Director of Line Extension and the Plant Quality Control Director are valuable ancillary players for the implementation plan to work. Not only are they good, fertile, critical thinkers, but having them in the session is politically expedient, too.

B. Look For Chinks In The Armor

Ask the group to generate as many ways as they can think of that the solution will fail. What kinds of situations can present themselves to undermine or render impossible the paths that you have chosen? How can a series of events occur that will make your situation more difficult than if you leave things as they are? The group might be reticent at first, but after a while, they will warm up and generate a formidable list. Analytical people love to be critical. Invite them to tear your solution apart.

POTENTIAL PCP OBSTACLES
(Partial list)

- The Vice President of Manufacturing might balk at spending the money.
- The motels around the plant might be over-booked.
- People might just refuse to cooperate with each other.
- Analysis of lost time might prove too difficult.
- Long-term fix might require major rebuild of machine.
- Technical consultant might not be available.
- Quality control group at the plant might be less effective because their space is reduced.
- The airlines might strike.
- The R&D people might be killed in a plane crash.
- New technology introduction by a competitor might put us further in the hole because of the refocus of R&D efforts.
- The union might sabotage the solution because the better the machine runs, the less overtime their people get.
- People might get disgruntled with the hard work and quit.

C. Determine Probability

Get information from all available sources as to the probability that each of these items in your list might actually occur. Rank order from the greatest probability to the least.

> PCP decided to break the objections into two groups. One group had an insignificantly small probability, e.g., plane crashes, and was not considered. The other group was significant and was considered below.

1. Analysis of lost time might prove too difficult.
2. Long-term fix might require major rebuild of machine.
3. Technical consultant might not be available.
4. New technology introduction by competitor might put us further in the hole because we are not operating normally.
5. The union may prove a difficult obstacle to the types of problem solving teams we are instituting.

D. Create "Plan B"

Assume the first occurrence happens. How might you modify your solution to take full advantage of it? Or how might you avoid being impacted by changing your solution? Use all the techniques you have learned so far to see the solution in a new way which takes care of the potential problem.

E. Generate More "Plan Bs"

Consider each potential negative occurrence and develop modifications that will protect, prepare, or help you to find some benefit in them, should they occur.

> PCP took a close look at each of these five potential roadblocks. The following example is the first one they considered. The rest of the potential obstacles can be found in Appendix E.

1. ANALYSIS OF LOST TIME MAY PROVE TOO DIFFICULT.

This is a problem because if we can't figure out what's causing the breakdown on the machines, we won't be able to develop any short-term fix. If this happens, we either shut the operation down and transfer everyone back to work in the lab, or do something else. The first option is not acceptable. We need to think about "something else." We might need to reinforce ourselves with consultants who can help us with the data analysis.

We have one consultant in the Technical Information Department at R&D. The V.P. of R&D will ask the Director of Technical Information to lend us this person for at least five months. It will give him a chance to shine.

We also need an expert in design experiments who can help us minimize the variables. There is a person who teaches a course in this at the local college. I think he would love to help us. We also need a computer expert to help us measure the machine condition data more frequently, making it easier for us to spot trends and see cause-effect relationships between machine conditions and performance. All of these consultants are available to us, which reduces this problem to a lower probability of occurrence.

F. Identify The Downside

There may be potential roadblocks which can not be countered. If you have any of these on your list, your downside risk is represented by the cumulative probability that these roadblocks will actually happen.

G. Value The Risk

Calculate the value of your risk by determining the total cost of the solution. Keep this number nearby. It will be used again at the end of the next section.

It seems that there are several basic additional costs to consider, aside from the basic expenses of relocation.

One is for the additional consultants needed to minimize the analysis problem. This costs approximately $100,000. Developing a working model of the machinery will cost us an additional $80,000, making the total additional expenditure for minimizing all the risks about $180,000.

The manpower charges for the shift involve eight people for an average of four months. That's two and two-thirds man years at $60,000 per year for a total of $160,000.

The motel, travel expenses, and meal expenses will be about $100,000. Redesigning the quality control lab will be about $40,000. This adds up to a downside risk of approximately $500,000.

IMPLEMENTATION PLAN — **MAXIMIZING GAIN**

1.   Mental Events Slide Show
2.   Activities List
3.   Activities Review
4.   Problem Activities
5.   Selling the Idea
6.   Developing Risk Insurance
→   **7.   MAXIMIZING GAIN**
8.   Attitude Checking
9.   Taking the First Step

OFTEN A SOLUTION PROVIDES OTHER UNEXPECTED RESULTS

Often, an innovative solution to an existing problem provides other, unexpected opportunities of equal or greater value than the positive benefit from just solving the problem. Problem solving in the space program, for example, has led to the development of Teflon® cookery, Velcro®, and many other devices that improve the quality of life for everyone. In the following section, we will look for ancillary opportunities that may exist as a result of our solution, as well as ways to capitalize on them. If we can find potentially profitable ventures linked to the problem solving you have done so far, they may help offset the risk you are about to undertake.

A. Restate the Problem

State your original problem in three sentences by describing the present situation.

PCP Example:

We have developed a new technology for diaper facing which allows us to be competitive. Although it has been a success in the lab and in market testing, we are unable to produce the facing successfully in commercial quantities. We need to develop a commercially successful technology and to have it in operation in six months.

B. State Major Insight

State what blockages you have successfully overcome with your solution. Or, you might want to state any major lessons you have learned from working on your problem. Look for a new, big-picture perspective that you have discovered in this process.

> PCP Example:
>
> Our inability to recognize that the way people work together is often more important to the success or failure of a project than any technical breakthrough made by a small group of isolated individuals.

C. Describe the Solution

Briefly describe your solution, paying attention specifically to the insights you have developed, as well as the changes of view you made to develop a successful resolution.

> PCP Example:
>
> The solution involves a multi-disciplinary team, each member with a different expertise and viewpoint, working together in an open, creative way to solve a specific problem. This is a creative problem solving team. (CPS Team)
>
> It is abundantly clear that when everyone is encouraged to express his or her point of view, and value can be extracted from each view, then the intelligence, power, and ultimate productivity of the group is far greater than the sum of the intellect of the individual group members. It is also clear that many problems disguising themselves as technical problems are in fact interpersonal difficulties.

D. General Principles

List some of the general principles or patterns that have emerged from your solutions that might be applicable elsewhere. Again, we are looking for major principles or guidelines you might tend to remember when working on another problem.

> PCP Example:
>
> 1. You can accomplish a great deal if you make your adversary your friend.
> 2. Regarding negative situations as creative challenges or potential positive resources can significantly increase your options for improving the business.

E. Additional Arenas

List all of the areas in which your business is involved that are not necessarily tied to your specific problem. If you have other product lines, list them. If your business is very diversified, list just four or five other products not involved in your problem. We are looking for other product-oriented areas of interest in your business that are not part of your immediate problem.

PCP Example:
1. Manufacture of plastic baby bottles.
2. Manufacture of disposable trash bags.
3. Research in new polymer technology for auto bodies.
4. Advanced product research in diapers.

F. Miscellaneous Areas

List *any* other areas of your business that do not necessarily depend on a successful resolution to this problem. Is there anything your business markets or is otherwise known for, that is not connected to your problem? If so, list it here.

PCP Example:
1. Development of new technologies.
2. Other baby comfort products.

G. Create A Wish List

Using other business colleagues, develop a "wish list" of additional opportunity areas in new products, changes to existing products, new methods for manufacturing, and challenges with which they are faced that are causing them concern.

PCP Example:
1. Zero inventory at warehouses.
2. Heightened morale and less employee turnover.
3. Three new product development breakthroughs this year.
4. Additional lower-cost sources of supply for polymer chemicals.

H. Create An Idea Matrix

1. Develop a two-dimensional matrix or graph. Across the top, place all the general principles, insights, new ideas, and procedures that you have developed for solving your problem. (Items from Steps C and D.)

2. On the left, from top to bottom, list all of the challenges that you have accumulated in Steps E, F, and G.

3. Fill in the internal boxes by forcing relationships between the challenges and the insights. Use the insights you have developed to help find opportunities in each of the ancillary challenge areas.

PCP EXAMPLE

	CPS Teams	Making your adversary your ally	Negative situations as positive resources
Baby Bottles	Panel of mothers for new ideas		
Disposable trash bags Automobile bodies		Consider using trash bags in compactors	
			Strands of metal reinforcing plastic
Advanced Diaper	Work more closely marketing		
Devel of New Hires	Develop mentor system perhaps using retirees of corp.		
Other comfort products		Take one of Robinson's products and make it more comfortable	
Zero inventory	Invite vendors to CPS session		
Morale	Use CPS teams in all business areas		
3 new product breakthroughs	Invite ideas from everyone		Develop new product list from need inventory of emerging markets.
Lower cost supplies			Purchase supplier company

I. Valuing Your Ideas

1. Choose the most promising of the matrix ideas and calculate its dollar value if it is realized.

2. Calculate the reward for solving your original problem successfully.

3. Estimate the probability for success of your solution for the original problem, then the success probability of this new opportunity.

4. Multiply the dollar amounts by the appropriate probability numbers.

5. Add all the numbers from the above calculation. This value is your potential gain for attempting to implement your solution.

If the value in step five compares favorably to the value of your potential risk, proceed to the final step before beginning the implementation.

If the comparison is unfavorable, do more risk minimization work, increase the gain by finding more areas of opportunity, or return to the biggest blockage and develop another solution.

PCP Example:

Forcing relationships in the matrix between "Disposable trash bags" and "Making your adversary your ally" leads to the idea of trash bags specifically made for use in trash compactors. The idea is to develop a trash bag with tear-resistant properties to make use of the increasing volume of trash compactors which seem to be slowly eroding our trash bag business.

---

1. The benefit to us would be $3.5 million per year.
2. Solving the diaper facing problem is worth $10 million per year.
3. The probability for success for diaper facing is 60%, or .60.
4. The probability for success of the trash bag is about 20%, or .20.
5. Potential Gain $= \$10 \text{ million} \times 0.6 = \$6 \text{ million}$
   $+ \$3.5 \text{ million} \times 0.2 = \$0.7 \text{ million}$

   Total Pot. Gain $=$ $\$6.7 \text{ million}$

The $6.7 million potential reward compares favorably with the $.5 million risk (see page 122). So it makes sense to go ahead.

IMPLEMENTATION PLAN — **ATTITUDE CHECKING**

1. Mental Events Slide Show
2. Activities List
3. Activities Review
4. Problem Activities
5. Selling the Idea
6. Developing Risk Insurance
7. Maximizing Gain
→ 8. **Attitude Checking**
9. Taking the First Step

As was mentioned earlier, implementation is hard work. It takes perseverance, single-mindedness, commitment, and an almost blind obsession to make the solution work. Someone once said, "It is your attitude, not your aptitude, that determines your altitude."

"It's your attitude, not your aptitude, that determines your altitude"

Your willingness to "hang in there" is as much a function of how you *feel* about what you are trying to accomplish as it is a function of your confidence in the numbers and the logic of the risk. It is, therefore, very important to make certain that both feelings and thoughts, right brain and left brain, are in alignment to insure personal success. Following is a final exercise to help you develop that alignment.

A. Attitude Check

How do you feel about your solution? Surely, you are a mixture of anticipation and fright, reluctance and enthusiasm, optimism and pessimism. But when you net everything out, what does your body tell you? If you can identify a general feeling, and you have difficulty equating this to a sense of personal "rightness or wrongness" about your specific situation, ask yourself when you have experienced this feeling before. Under what conditions have you had this sense, and what happened as a result? It may help to take time away from the situation, and ask yourself these questions after you have had a chance to let your new ideas incubate. If you are feeling positive about the situation, skip the rest of this section and proceed to the last implementation step.

> PCP Example:
>
> The Research Manager said, "I feel generally positive about this, but there is a part of me that is reluctant to proceed. It's like the way I felt when I was a kid and wanted to start my own newspaper route. To get the route, I needed a bicycle and, not having any money, had to ask my parents to lend it to me. Well, it became a bigger hassle than I was prepared for, but I finally ended up getting the bike. However, my school work started making heavy demands and I wanted to play high school freshman baseball, so in a couple months, I gave up the the paper route."

If after having "slept on it," you are still unsure or feeling vaguely unsettled, proceed and see if the following steps make you feel better about your decision.

B. What's Affecting You?

One of several things could be causing your unsettled feelings. There is an activity or group of activities in your Activities List that are highly critical or more important to you than all of the others. Please revisit Section Two and mark the activities that are clearly the most important to you. Limit yourself to no more than five. Choose all of the marked items with a rating of two, and use problem solving techniques to raise them to a three.

PCP Example:

(The full text of this step can be found in Appendix E.) After much thought, the Research Manager decided that his problem was "How to minimize the downside risk to his career if the project failed."

By using the process of developing ideas for this "How to. . .", picking the best, defining what's useful about it, what's missing in it, and filling the gaps, the Research Manager decided the key to his problem would be in getting the Marketing Vice President totally committed to the solution, and involved in the problem solving necessary to make it work. The Marketing V.P., if he is involved in the project, will not allow it to fail.

C. Re-evaluation

How do you feel about your solution now? If you feel positive, proceed to the final step. If you are still unsettled, perhaps there is a criterion for your personal success or well-being that you have not articulated or that has not been satisfactorily addressed.

To determine whether or not this is the case, again consider when you have had these unsettled feelings before. Let yourself freely associate about other important decisions you have made that have not turned out the way you hoped. What was missing for you? How might you have changed things to reverse the outcome? How might you apply the learning that came from that situation to your current problem? What is it going to take in terms of satisfying those missing elements to make you more positive? How might you modify your sequence to take this into account?

D. Going For It

If after all this introspection you still feel uncomfortable, we urge you to plunge ahead, anyway. Assuming you have honestly and wholeheartedly used this process and invested this much effort, the chances of utter failure have been minimized. And finally, you never want to face the empty experience of looking back and saying "I should have. . ."

A final thought from Ralph Waldo Emerson in "Self-Reliance:"

> *To believe your own thought, to believe that what is true for you in your private heart, is true for all men, that is genius. Speak your latent convictions, and it shall be the universal sense; for always the inmost, in due time becomes the outmost — Else, tomorrow a stranger will say with masterly good sense, precisely what we have thought and felt all the time, and we shall be forced to take with shame our own opinion from another.*

IMPLEMENTATION PLAN — **TAKING THE FIRST STEP**

    1.   Mental Events Slide Show
    2.   Activities List
    3.   Activities Review
    4.   Problem Activities
    5.   Selling the Idea
    6.   Developing Risk Insurance
    7.   Maximizing Gain
    8.   Attitude Checking
→   **9.   TAKING THE FIRST STEP**

You are prepared. It is now time to take the most important step, the first one. This is the one move that overcomes the inertia and sets things in motion. Pay special attention to it. Celebrate it.

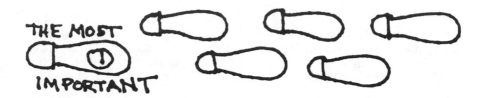

What follows are a series of suggestions that may help to make the first step successful.

1. List all of the people involved in taking the first step.

2. From your knowledge of them and their thinking styles, how might you present your idea to them so they might put high priority on doing what you would like them to?

3. When might be the best time to approach them?

4. To establish momentum, determine locations, circumstances, and places that will maximize your chances of getting buy-in.

5. Finally, on a blank piece of paper, write a simple declarative statement:
   "I will _____ by _____."

Sign it, date it, and hang it in a prominent place in your office or home.

The PCP example of this final step may be found in Appendix E.

Remember, if anything unforeseen happens, you still have a huge resource on which you can depend: your own creative energies and your willingness to change problems into opportunities. Your creativity is infinite. It is limited only by the strength of your attitude and your commitment to live a creative life.

Where do the stars end?

Creativity is like that — infinite!

Solving Impossible Problems

Advanced Creative Techniques

THE PARADOX BOX

I wouldn't want to join any club that would have me as a member.

— Groucho

Have you ever gotten that old "can't get there from here" feeling? Have you ever looked at your problem and decided that you are not on the same planet with the rest of your group since what has been asked of you is simply impossible?

"What do you mean cut my resources by 15 percent and increase my productivity by 20 percent? Are you crazy?"

To those unenlightened in creative thinking, things are either black or white. As one becomes more experienced, things appear more often in shades of gray. But to the truly creative person, it is quite possible for things to be both black and white at the same time.

A friend, a professor at The City University of New York, relates a powerful personal experience. While serving in the Pacific during World War II, the professor's unit entered Nagasaki two weeks after the bomb was dropped. The utter destruction and desolation appalled him. Everything he saw was charred and blackened. Fires started spontaneously. Everywhere, bodies lay strewn among the rubble.

Then he lifted his eyes up about ten degrees above the horizon, and before him he saw the most sublime, breath-taking sunset he had ever seen. The simultaneous existence of those two conflicting realities was one of the most powerful and moving experiences of his life.

Paradox is a simple fact of life. If you ever drive on Route 128 around Boston, you will notice two route signs, mounted one over the other on the same pole. They read: 95 North and Rt. 128 South. When you read this sign, you will be traveling due east.

Things which seem to be mutually exclusive do often co-exist. Our relationships with significant others embrace love and hate, boredom and excitement, clarity and obscurity, all at once. Anyone who has eaten jumbo shrimp, worked in military intelligence, or hired a creative consultant has had firsthand experience with paradox.

In fact, paradox often works as the catalyst for the creative process. Understanding that contradictory and "illogical" systems can exist in harmony lies at the heart of solving problems creatively. In problem-solving terms, paradox is mutually contradicting present and future states that apparently make the gap between them insurmountable. Finding remote connections by dealing with the paradox in a positive and nourishing way might develop additional perceptions about the situation, taking us where we want to go.

If you have been working on your own problem through this book, and it still is not resolved, quite possibly you are caught in the paradox box — a dead end at every turn.

Whenever you have an unbridgeable gap with paradox boxing you in, the solution hides in a totally different approach. Your point of view must change, allowing you to look at it from a completely new perspective.

This chapter offers three different techniques for the perceptual changes needed to resolve paradoxical problems. Each technique is self-contained: you may use any one of them without the other two.

The three techniques are:

1. THE LOGICAL PARADOX — defining and *using* the paradoxical nature of your situation to develop new perspectives for a successful resolution.
2. GREAT MINDS INVENTORY — using the knowledge and wisdom accumulated through the ages to help you consider your situation differently.
3. ASSUMPTION REVERSAL — Developing new and potentially more beneficial perspectives by discovering the unconscious, fundamental assumptions behind your paradox and systematically reversing them.

BACKGROUND

In 1981, a study in the *Journal of Creative Behavior* attempted to describe the thought process creative people experience when they receive a new insight or idea. The people chosen for the study had two characteristics in common: they were considered by their peers to be creative; and they remembered their creative episodes moment by moment and could report in detail what occurred.

Interestingly, an astounding percentage of those surveyed reported similarities in the sequence of their creative process. The following relates the steps they described in getting ideas for a long-standing problem or challenge.

1. I get an image (a mental picture) of an item, group of items, or experience that has piqued my interest. (At this point there is no conscious relationship

between this image and the resolution to some inner problem, conflict, or challenge.)

2. The image becomes "fuzzy" or out of focus.

3. I lose the image momentarily, almost like a mental blink.

4. A new image appears, and this picture depicts the successful resolution of some problem or challenge I've been wrestling with.

From this study, it seems to us that there are two critical elements to solving problems creatively: first, *the ability to create internal mental images;* and second, *the ability to fuzz, distort, or soften these images.*

The techniques in this chapter present you with fresh images about the problem, as well as ways of fuzzing or distorting them.

LOGICAL PARADOX

This technique helps you identify the logical paradox of your situation and label it with an appropriate oxymoron. In case you don't remember, an oxymoron is a figure of speech combining two contradictory terms, such as our title for this technique — Logical Paradox.

Once an appropriate oxymoron has been found, we look for other examples of that same oxymoron in different situations, and using our Forced Relationship Form, we develop opportunities leading to implementable solutions.

We have used this technique many times. One which comes to mind was with a major manufacturer of paper towels. We will call the company Fabulaire.

THE STORY

Fabulaire began losing their market share to other companies who had developed technical modifications making their towels more functional than Fabulaire's. Consumers, who had been loyal, were slowly switching to the competitor, R&B Paper. Due to limited technical resources, Fabulaire was unable to develop a towel that could functionally compete with R&B's improvements.

The two assets that Fabulaire had vis-a-vis R&B were that they manufactured their towels at an extremely high speed, thereby reducing fixed costs and enabling their product to be cost competitive, and their highly advanced decorating equipment allowed them to emboss and print more sophisticated graphics on their towels.

After examining all of the ideas for leveraging their assets to help them regain market share, they invited us to help. They wanted a creative session to make sure that they had not missed an exciting opportunity.

The following material outlines each step of the Logical Paradox process.

DESCRIBING THE PROBLEM — FUTURE

The beginning of this technique requires the same information as the beginning of Kaleidoscope. If you have worked through the Kaleidoscope process, use the information you generated in its first section for the following steps A - C.

A. Imagine Your Problem Is Solved

If you have not worked through Kaleidoscope, begin by sitting back, relaxing, and imagining that you have found a solution to your problem, that you have started implementing it, and the solution is working. Take some time to get a good picture in your mind of what that experience might be like.

B. Who Is Involved?

Make a Forced Relationship Form. On the left side, in the Key Column, list all of the people who are directly or indirectly involved in implementing your solution. Be sure to include anyone who might be directly or indirectly influencing the implementation process. List names; positions, i.e., the VP of Manufacturing; or categories of people, such as customers, suppliers, technicians. This is another time when quantity is important. Don't leave *anyone* out. And remember, this is an opportunity to have things exactly as you want them. Let your imagination go.

> In the following Fabulaire example, we have included a few of those that were listed to show the diversity of people who should be on this list.

FABULAIRE EXAMPLE

(Key Column) People Involved	(Insight Column)
Female Paper Towel Purchaser Productin People Marketing People	

FABULAIRE EXAMPLE (CONTINUED)

(Key Column) People Involved	(Insight Column)
Financial People Advertising People Supermarkets Salespeople Color & Design Consultants CoCo Channel	

C. What Are They Doing?

Continue assuming that everything in this imaginary future is exactly as you want it to be. Look at the people in your Key Column one by one and imagine what they are doing in the implementation of your solution. How are they behaving? What role are they playing? List what they are doing in the Insight Column opposite their entry in the Key Column.

> Although the following example lists only one activity for each involved person, you may actually have two or three (or more) activities for each one. The greater the *quantity* you generate here, the better your opportunities for finding high *quality* ideas later in the process.

FABULAIRE EXAMPLE:

(Key Column) People Involved	(Insight Column) What they are doing
Female Paper Towel Purchaser	She is excited about looking forward to the next purchase of Fabulaire Towels.
Production People	They're so excited about the new hand towels, they're buying them for their families.
Marketing People	Marketing people have found a way to turn on the individual consumer.
Financial People	Financial people are developing much greater bottom line results as we reach new consumers.
Advertising People	Have found a new way to appeal to consumers that is a perceived added value to the towel.
Supermarkets	Supermarket owners are giving Fabulaire more shelf space than they had before.
Salespeople	Salespeople are so swamped with orders that they're putting their clients on allotment.
Color & Design Consultants	Color and design consultants have made the towel particularly appealing to the interests of the consumer.
CoCo Channel	CoCo Channel has told us that to be irreplaceable, one must be different.

D. Select Interesting Items

Look through all your entries in the Insight Column and check all that you feel might be relevant to a successful resolution or that interest you in any way. You do not have to know how to make that result happen, only that it would be particularly useful or intriguing.

> In the Fabulaire example, they checked four activities they found either important or interesting.

✓   Marketing people have found a way to turn on the individual consumer.

✓   Financial people are developing much greater bottom line results as we reach new people.

✓   Color and design consultants have made the towel particularly appealing to the interests of the consumer.

✓   CoCo Channel has told us that to be irreplaceable, one must be different.

E. Find Essence Words

Read through each statement you have checked as interesting or important. If you had to reduce that list down to a series of one-word statements, what would they be? Create a list of these words which somehow capture the essence, feeling, or intent of your checked items. Later we will refer to this list as the Future Essence Words.

Fabulaire Example:

Unique
Individual
Exciting
Value
Different

DESCRIBING THE PROBLEM — PRESENT

The next steps ask you to create, by considering your present situation, a second list of "essence" words that are antonyms of the list you just created. We will call this list the Present Essence Words. Finally, we will make a third list, a list of oxymorons by pairing the Future and the Present Essence Word lists.

A. Describe Your Current Situation

Write a brief description of your situation as it exists today. (3-5 sentences)

Fabulaire Example:

Fabulaire's paper towel is being made technically obsolete by new product improvements from other towel manufacturers. Fabulaire is slowly losing market share because consumers are switching to competitive products. We are becoming a "me too" commodity item.

B. What Have You Tried?

What have you already tried to resolve this problem, and why do you think it has failed? If this is your first shot at resolving the situation, why do you think it needs a creative solution?

Fabulaire Example:

We have tried to catch up technically, but we don't have the research resources. We have also tried to capitalize on our decorating expertise, to appeal to the consumer, but so far, the ideas we have come up with aren't sufficient to carve out a unique niche in the market place.

C. Create An Antonym List

Look at your description of the current situation, and develop a second list of one-word statements that are antonyms of your Future Essence Words. Specifically, you are looking for words capturing the difference between the present situation and the situation in the future when the problem is solved. This list is your Present Essence Words.

Fabulaire Example:

Average
Mediocre
Mass
Same

D. Combine Lists

Couple each of your Present Essence Words with each of your Future Essence Words. Take the first word from the present list and the second word from the future list.

Fabulaire Example:

average - unique	mediocre - unique	mass - unique	same - unique
average - exciting	mediocre - exciting	mass - exciting	same - exciting
average - different	mediocre - different	mass - different	same - different
average - individual	mediocre - individual	mass - individual	same - individual
average - value	mediocre - value	mass - value	same - value

E. Change To Adjective — Noun Phrase

Change your two words into a phrase where the first word is an adjective and the second is a noun. Now you have a list of oxymorons grown directly from your situation.

Fabulaire Example:

average - uniqueness	mediocre - uniqueness	mass - uniqueness	same - uniqueness
average - excitement	mediocre - excitement	mass - excitement	same - excitement
average - difference	mediocre - difference	mass - difference	same - difference
average - individuality	mediocre - individuality	mass - individuality	same - individuality
average - value	mediocre - value	mass - value	same - value

F. Choose The Best Oxymoron

Look over the list of oxymorons you have just created, and choose one which best captures the paradox of your present and future situations.

Fabulaire Example:

mass uniqueness

THE ANALOGOUS IMAGE

Now that you have an appropriate oxymoron, you can put it to work for you. Think of your oxymoron as a bridge that can carry you from you present situation into your future situation. In this section you will find a real-world example of your paradox and use it to stimulate ideas for your problem.

A. Find A Parallel World

In Appendix D you will find a list of "parallel worlds." This is a list of areas of life or history such as the worlds of sports or Greek history. Study the list and find a world which contains in it a working example of your paradox. The Fabulaire case illustrates this difficult-to-explain step perfectly.

Fabulaire Example:

Fabulaire chose the "World Of Fashion." Thinking about the "World Of Fashion" brought them to the *make-up mirror*, which is an example of mass uniqueness. The mirror is the same for everyone, but at the same time everyone sees a unique reflection in it.

> Note: What is important in this step is that you find a working example of your paradox. Sometimes you may think of an example without looking through the list of parallel worlds. Other times you may find the list helpful in unlocking ideas for examples.

B. Set Up A Forced Relationship Form

In a Forced Relationship Form, put the example from your parallel world over the Key Column, and put the phrase: "How to develop (your two-word paradox)" over the Insight Column.

Fabulaire Example:

(Key Column) A Make-up Mirror	(Insight Column) How to Develop Mass Uniqueness

C. List Characteristics

List as many unique characteristics of your example as possible in the Key Column. Look for those elements which are particularly representative of your example.

This is another opportunity to go for quantity. While our example shows only seven entries, in reality there were many, many more. The more characteristics you can think of, the better your chances are of discovering a unique insight.

Fabulaire Example:

(Key Column) A Make-up Mirror	(Insight Column) How to Develop Mass Uniqueness
People see themselves closeup. Image is reflection of real person. It allows each person to focus on their individual attributes. It is made of glass. Highlights positive characteristics of individuals. People can see transformation. It is personal and private.	

D. Complete The Forced Relationship

As you have throughout the book, use the unique characteristics in the Key Column to unlock insights in the Insight Column.

Remember that each entry in the Key Column may stimulate more than one idea in the Insight Column. Try to let your ideas flow.

Fabulaire Example:

(Key Column) A Make-up Mirror	(Insight Column) How to Develop Mass Uniqueness
People see themselves closeup	Put shiny wrapper on product.
Image is reflection of real person.	Put people's names on towels.
It allows each person to focus on their individual attributes.	Listing of positive attributes of different types of people.
It is made of glass.	Use reflective decorations.
Highlights positive characteristics of individuals.	Present only the positive side of things.
People can see transformation.	A decoration that changes people's attitudes.
It is personal and private.	People feel that the towel decoration is speaking to them individually.

E. Pick The Best Idea

Looking through the Insight Column, check the idea that has the greatest potential for solving your problem. Don't worry if you do not know how to do it now. We work on making the idea practical next.

Fabulaire Example: ✓ List the positive attributes of specific types of individuals.

143

F. Find What Is Useful, Solve What Is Missing

Using the technique of Dissecting Ideas from Chapter Two, describe what is useful about the idea you chose, what is missing in it, and fill the missing gaps with ideas.

> This is your opportunity to make your chosen idea practical. Be certain not to limit your imagination and miss a chance to make a good idea real. List plenty of ideas when the process gives you the opportunity. Our example below is an abridged version.

Fabulaire Example:

What's Useful? (about listing the positive attributes of specific types of individuals on the towels.)

1. Makes people feel good.
2. Develops personal identification with the brand.
3. Potential ancillary spin-off with other disposable items.

What's Missing?

How to describe specific types of people that are general enough to be mass produced but personal enough so everyone can individually identify.

Ideas

1. Use signs of the Zodiac.
2. Use personality types from psychology.

Idea #1

Use signs of the Zodiac to develop twelve different decorations, each listing attributes of the sign.

What's Useful?

1. Develops mass manufacturing technique.
2. Establishes unique identification.
3. Capitalizes on astrological interests of consumers.

What's Missing?

How to develop repeat sales?

Ideas

1. Include an astrological guide for each month, listing what's productive for the individual during that time.

What's Useful?

1. Develops repeat sales.
2. People look forward to buying the towels each month.
3. Provides topic for conversation when people get together.

What's Missing?

How to include a monthly astrological forecast?

Ideas

1. Hire a famous astrologer to write forecasts each month and include these in the towel wrapper.

What's Useful?

1. Totally solves the problem.
2. Makes people feel that Fabulaire is interested in their individual fortunes.
3. Develops personal connection between Fabulaire and the individual consumer.

What's Missing?

Nothing!

ADDITIONAL THOUGHTS

Paradox represents a powerful opportunity for creative problem solving. Some of the most creative and profitable inventions of our time have evolved from it. For example, look at Velcro™ and 3M's Post-It™ Notes. Both commercial blockbusters embody the paradox: *temporary permanence*. These products easily embrace those seemingly contradictory qualities, which appear so sensible once the paradox is solved.

"Of course," you say, slapping your forehead, "why didn't I think of that?"

You didn't think of it because the *logical* connection between temporary and permanent did not exist in a real, tangible way before actually seeing an example of it. Undaunted by the paradox, the inventors were challenged to create a connection. And once found, a new order existed and new logic was formed. The logic became obvious to all, creating sore foreheads all over the world.

So if paradox appears in your life, embrace the challenge. You have an opportunity to make history. Use the Logical Paradox technique, or the two following techniques, to discover the new connection.

THE GREAT MINDS INVENTORY

We cannot stress enough that the single greatest creative skill lies in the ability to see key elements of a solution in seemingly disassociated ideas or concepts. And the more disassociated, such as in a paradox, the greater the opportunity for finding creative solutions.

"If you put a chain around the neck of a slave, the other end attaches to your own"

EMERSON

The Great Minds Inventory provides a method for gaining new insight into your most difficult problems by forcing a relationship between a problem and quotations from history's greatest thinkers. In addition, this technique capitalizes on the fact that different people tend to think in different styles, and so it consciously asks you to think in a way which is not your preferred style. If you are an Analyzer, you might choose to consider the problem from the point of view of a Collaborator. Or if you are an Imaginator, you might try on the Implementor's hat. Why do something abnormal for you? Because your normal modes of thinking have not solved the problem. The problem demands something radically new and different.

Like many of our other techniques in this book, the Great Minds Inventory draws heavily on your ability to force relationships. If you are not an expert by now, you have not been reading this book through from the beginning. If you need brushing up on making forced relationships, revisit Chapter Two for review and practice.

PREPARATION

Are you an Analyzer, Implementor, Collaborator, or Imaginator? Of the Four Faces of Creativity, which is the one you most prefer? If you haven't yet taken the short test to determine your thinking style in Appendix C, try it now. The Great Minds Inventory depends on you knowing your own style.

The Great Minds Inventory works on the concept that problems demand different kinds of solutions. What happens when you are an Analyzer who prefers logical and analytical thinking, and your problem demands a solution which calls for the empathetic, interpersonal thinking of the Collaborator? Since the Collaborator and the Analyzer are diametric opposites, it is possible that the collaborative solution would completely elude you.

This same situation may prevail *whenever* the solution lies in a thinking style for which you have very little preference. Your least preferred area will be the last place you look, especially if your preference in that area is particularly low. It's only natural. Your least preferred area can seem like alien territory. The Great Minds Inventory offers an expert guide to take you into that jungle where your solution may have been hiding all along.

A NEW STORY

A major public utility company in the Northeast has run into significant operating problems. Historically, if people did not pay their gas bills for heating, the gas company cut off their gas. It was that simple. Without gas, these families, mostly lower to middle income people, were quick to arrange payment of their delinquent bills.

Since many of the negligent families heated with gas, this technique was especially effective in the winter months. They usually found a way to pay something toward their bill to keep the heat on.

Then a new law was passed making it illegal for the gas company to turn off gas to delinquent accounts between October and May. That was it! All the people who were only paying their gas bill to stay warm, put it at the bottom of the pile.

It was clear from our analysis that poor families used more gas per capita than other groups, perhaps because their homes were so poorly constructed. The other problem compounding the issue was that natural gas prices had risen, making gas more difficult to afford. To prevent a huge deficit, the gas company increased the charges to residential accounts to offset those who were not paying their bills.

This further enraged residential customers who were paying their bills, and who were suffering the burden of the higher natural gas prices. They, too, became delinquent accounts in protest of what they saw as an arbitrary and inhumane action by the gas company. They threatened to file suit against the company. Things quickly became critical for the utility. The situation had to change. It was at this point that we were invited to work on the problem.

Using the Great Minds Inventory, here is what the president of the gas company came up with.

OPENING

If you have been working on a problem through the course of the book, simply borrow your description from "Describing the Problem" in

Kaleidoscope from Chapter Three. If you have not already described your problem somewhere else, or if you are starting a new problem, continue with the questions below.

A. Describe The Problem

Write a brief (3-5 sentences) description of the problem.

Utility Example:

With the increase in gas prices, it's become increasingly difficult to get residential accounts to pay. Compounding the problem, a new law makes it illegal to turn gas service off for residential customers from October to May. Attempts at passing the increased operating costs on to the customer base have met with stiff opposition, making everything worse.

B. What Have You Tried?

What have you already tried to resolve this problem, and why do you think it has failed? If this is your first shot at resolving the situation, why do you think it needs a creative solution?

Utility Example:

There doesn't seem to be any leveraging position we can take to force delinquent accounts to pay their bills.

C. What Do You Stand To Lose?

Imagine that you don't resolve this problem. What is at stake? What do you stand to lose?

Utility Example:

I will probably lose my job!

D. What Do You Stand To Gain?

Next, if you don't resolve the problem, is there anything you stand to gain? Try to think of some advantage the status quo would offer.

Utility Example:

I will be free to pursue other careers that might be more lucrative and cause less frustration.

E. Summarize With A "How to. . ."

Summarize what needs to be changed in your situation in one statement beginning with the words "How to. . . ."

Utility Example:

How to get residential accounts to pay their gas bills.

EXPLORING GREAT MINDS

Now that you have narrowed your problem down to a one-sentence "How to. . ." statement, we can force relationships to find answers for it. The following steps take you through a Forced Relationship process using your problem and a quotation from one of the world's greatest thinkers to stimulate new ideas for your difficult problem.

A. Create A Forced Relationship Form

Draw a Forced Relationship Form and write your "How to. . ." statement over the Insight Column.

Utility Example:

(Key Column)	(Insight Column) How to get residential accounts to pay their gas bill.

B. Find Your Lowest Score

Look at your scores from the Personal Style Inventory. You should have four numerical values. In which column did you score the lowest, i.e., Analyzer, Implementor, Collaborator, Imaginator?

Utility Example:

My lowest score is Collaborator.

C. Pick A Number

Think of any number between one and fifteen.

Utility Example:

Three

D. Find Your Quote

Turn to Appendix B. In this appendix, we have listed a series of 60 quotations. These quotes are organized into four groups of fifteen for each of the four thinking styles. For example, quotations in the Analyzer's section were either made by Analyzers, or are representative of the kinds of logical, analytical thinking common to an Analyzer.

Turn to the area in which you scored the lowest in the Personal Styles Inventory (your least preferred style), and find the quotation with the number corresponding to your random number.

Utility Example:

The Utility president's least preferred style was the Collaborator. His random number was three. Quotation #3 in the Collaborator section is:

If you put a chain around the neck of a slave, the other end fastens to your own.

—Emerson

E. Put Quote In Forced Relationship Form

Next, write the quotation in the Key Column of your Forced Relationship Form.

Utility Example:

(Key Column) ''If you put a chain around the neck of a slave, the other end fastens to your own.''	(Insight Column) How to get residential accounts to pay their gas bill.

F. Fill-In The Key Column

What thoughts, ideas, and comments does the quote elicit for you? Think about the quote and write what comes to mind as entries in the Key Column.

> Don't let yourself be intimidated by the quote or the process. There aren't any wrong answers here. Let your mind play with the quote and all its implications for you. Most importantly, don't censor yourself. No one is going to see this work, so write as many entries as you can.

Utility Example:

(Key Column) ''If you put a chain around the neck of a slave, the other end fastens to your own.''	(Insight Column) How to get residential accounts to pay their gas bill.
Slaves had chains around their necks. To be free, you have to free other people. A slave can pull you around. If the chain is heavy, it can drag you down. The more slaves you have, the heavier the burden. Emerson wrote a monologue on self-reliance. Cutting the ties that bind makes you free. Heavy chains are metal.	

G. Fill-In The Insight Column

Look at each of your entries in the Key Column. What association or relationship can you make between your thoughts about the quotation and ways to solve your "How to. . ." in the Insight Column? Try to make *at least* one entry in the Insight Column for every entry in the Key Column.

> Stay loose with your thinking. Don't try for the one blockbuster idea, just let all ideas come at their own pace. Don't try. Relax. Trust the process.

Utility Example:

(Key Column) "If you put a chain around the neck of a slave, the other end fastens to your own."	(Insight Column) How to get residential accounts to pay their gas bill.
Slaves had chains around their necks. To be free, you have to free other people. A slave can pull you around. If the chain is heavy, it can drag you down. The more slaves you have, the heavier the burden. Emerson wrote a monologue on self-reliance. Cutting the ties that bind makes you free. Heavy chains are metal.	1. Chain up their gas heaters. 2. Make gas free for all people. 3. Talk to delinquent accounts to find out why they don't pay. 4. Help people with their problems. 5. Help switch to another form of energy. 6. Help people not to depend on gas heat. 7. Quit my job. 8. Try sending delinquents to jail.

H. Pick The Best Idea

Look through all the ideas in your Insight Column and pick the idea or combination of ideas which you find exciting and which hold the most promise for you. Then dissect your idea, looking for what is useful about it and what is missing in it. Finally, restate what is missing in terms of a "How to. . ." statement.

> If, after looking through all your ideas in the Insight Column, there aren't any ideas you find particularly interesting, go to Step I below.

Utility Example:

The utility president chose to combine ideas 4 and 5: Help people to depend less heavily on gas heat.

Useful
- It would cut their bills.
- It would free up money to pay for other things.
- It would lower natural gas prices.
- People would erase their bad credit ratings.

Missing
How to help people cut down on their gas consumption?

I. Compare Statements Or Situations

There is still something missing. If you have found an idea and dissected it, then you have a new problem statement beginning with "How to. . ." representing what is missing in your solution to your problem.

If you have forced the relationship with the quote and not found an interesting idea in the Insight Column, then there is something missing in each of the notions you developed.

The nature of what is missing can help you as you try to fill the gaps in your particular problem. If you have developed a new problem statement, continue with Step 1. If you did not get an idea by forcing the relationship, then go to Step 2.

1. For Those With An Idea

Look at your new problem statement. Which of the four statements below best represents the kinds of ideas you need?

a.   I need ideas which are consistent with my analysis of the core issues. They need to fit the data.

b.   I need ideas for developing procedures and plans. I need control over key issues.

c.   I need ideas that deal with people problems or the cooperation of some key individual.

d.   I need ideas that will give me exciting and stimulating new perceptions. I need to find something unique.

2. For Those Without An Idea

Look through the ideas you did generate in the Insight Column. There is something missing in each of them, preventing them from being exciting for you. If you could summarize what is missing in one sentence, which of the four statements below comes the closest to expressing the problem with your ideas?

a.   All of the ideas I have been able to generate don't seem consistent with my analysis of the core issues, or I still can't see a logical relationship between the ideas and a viable solution to my problem. They just don't seem to fit the data.

b.   My ideas seem too complex or vague to develop procedures and plans for implementation. I feel like I don't have enough control over key issues.

c.   There seems to be a personal problem with the ideas I've generated. I need the cooperation of key individual(s) inaccessible to me.

d.   There is nothing exciting or stimulating about the ideas I've been able to develop. It seems like the same old rut I've been in before.

Utility Example:
The utility president felt he needed ideas that were consistent with the data he had on the energy consumption for the families they service. He picked statement A.

J. Pick A New Number

Choose another number between one and fifteen. If you picked statement a. in the previous step, get your numbered quote from the Analyzer's list. If you picked statement b., get your quote from the Organizer's list. If you picked statement c., go to the Collaborator's list. And if you picked statement d., use the Imaginator's list.

Utility Example:
The number picked was four, and the fourth quotation from the Analyzer's list was:

One should not confuse the painter, the painting, and the easel.

—Bhagavad Gita

K. A New Forced Relationship

Place the new quote over the Key Column and the new problem statement over the Insight Column. Then work the Forced Relationship for new ideas for your problem statement in the Insight Column.

Utility Example:

(Key Column) "One should not confuse the painter, the painting, and the easel."	(Insight Column) How to help people cut their gas consumption.
The person who does the painting is the most important.	1. Find out why people use so much heat.
Break things down into components.	2. Look for all the reasons people use heat.
Going to the most basic thing gives people the greatest openness.	3. Look at the openings in people's homes.
The painting gives the easel meaning.	4. Supplying heat makes people want it.
The painter gives the painting meaning.	5. Show people that I'm human and care about their problems.
Lautrec painted on tablecloths.	6. Have coffee and make friends with delinquents.
The easel must be made ready to accept the painting.	7. Help people to change the way they do things to cut down on heat.
Greatest painters aren't recognized until after they die.	8. Shut down the gas company so people appreciate our problems.
Great paintings need to be in a protected environment to withstand the elements.	9. Weatherstrip big heat loss areas.

L. Pick An Idea

Look through your list in the Insight Column and choose and idea or combine ideas that move you toward a solution.

> If, while looking through the ideas, a new one comes to you, add it to the list. Don't feel you have to accept the ideas as you have originally worded them. Reading them through may stimulate a totally new notion that is what you're looking for.

Utility Example:
Combine 1, 2, 7, 9: Help people to make their environment use less heat.

M. Repeat

Using this new refinement of your idea, repeat Steps H-L.

Utility Example:

(H.) *Useful* (about helping people to make their environment use less heat).

- They use less gas, save money for same level of comfort.
- Makes them think of the gas company as their friend.
- Lowers the amount of money that we can't collect.

Missing

How to help people with limited funds to insulate their homes.

(I.) This "How to. . ." statement relates closest to Statement C in Step I-1. Choose a quote from the Collaborator List.

(J.) Quote:

> If two logs are dry and one is wet, the kindling of the two will kindle the wet one too.
>
> — Talmud

(K.)

(Key Column) If two logs are dry and one is wet, the kindling of the two will kindle the wet one too.	(Insight Column) How to help people with limited funds insulate their homes.
Things that have can help things that have not. Logs are found in the forest. Heat is more powerful than moisture.	1. Get the bank to loan people money. 2. Use neighborhood banks. 3. Show people we're genuinely interested in their problems.
Two is stronger than one. Using the potential of the strong will bring out the potential of the weak. Logs are used in a fireplace. You need wood chips to kindle logs.	4. Give examples of cost savings. 5. Underwrite loans to people. 6. Provide a free analysis of all heat sources. 7. Make sure interest rates are low.

(L.) Final idea a combination of 1, 5, and 6.

Provide low cost weatherization programs for delinquent accounts as well as ways they can cut their costs by insulating themselves. Not only does this go a long way in solving the problem, but it also gives us great PR in the city. There's nothing big missing.

THE REST OF THE STORY

This low cost weatherization program was actually put into action in a major U.S. city, and over time, it turned the gas company's losses around. It also performed an important and needed service to the city. The president, however, left the gas company after a couple of years and went into the private sector to get better mileage from his newly found creative talents.

SUMMARY

By tapping the techniques presented in Chapter Two, it is possible to access the thoughts and concepts of people who throughout the ages have been struggling with the same types of paradoxical issues that face us in our daily business lives. These ideas, if used properly, can help us to change the perceptions that tend to inhibit our thinking.

If you think a problem can't be solved, the first challenge is to understand that you're wrong. The problem simply presents the illusion of impossibility. Without this initial perceptual leap, chances are slim that you will ever be able to travel the rest of the distance to a solution. But those who do understand that there is at least one solution to every problem, are those who will solve them and gain reward in return.

Don't be daunted by the intricacy of any of these procedures. They need not be followed rigorously to produce results. The next time you experience a confict at business or even home, turn your least preferred thinking style (the one in which you scored the lowest), choose a number, and see if you can gain fresh insight from your choice.

ASSUMPTION REVERSAL

TIME FLIES NOT I THEY FLY TOO FAST

Read this statement. Punctuate it in such a way that the sentence makes complete sense.

The reason people find this problem difficult is that they make certain assumptions about the words. Once those assumptions are abolished, the solution becomes apparent, and we have more sore foreheads.

This, of course, holds true for all creative challenges. The problem may seem impossible because certain elements are believed to be inviolable truths. These elements are so fundamental, we never think to question them. However, once the assumption is challenged, light bulbs flash all over the place.

There is a famous story about a manufacturing group who packaged a metallic tube in oil soaked rags to protect it from damage and corrosion. They had been doing this successfully for about six years. The profit margin on the tubes was not very high, but they made money in volume.

Suddenly, with the oil embargo, the price of this oil increased significantly, and the group was forced into considering raising their prices to stay profitable. They met to brainstorm a solution. Dead ends loomed everywhere until someone asked what would happen if they used no protecting material. Guess what? The group discovered that about three years before, there had been a change in the metallic composition of the tubes where they no longer required the type of protection that was being used.

All of them had been laboring under an assumption that they needed the rags because that was the way it had always worked in the past. Once they reversed this assumption, the problem was easy to solve.

Look at another example. For quite a while, physicists had been aware that about six miles up in space, small particles called mesons are created. These particles all disintegrate in a very short period of time, and virtually none would be expected to reach the surface of the earth. However, when the meson concentration at the surface was measured, it was much higher than could be explained. How could so many of these particles get to the surface or survive if their life span was so short?

There seemed to be a paradox. The explanation and resolution of this apparent impossibility occurred when the scientists questioned a basic assumption — that time was absolute, and that the time the meson was experiencing was the same that the earth was experiencing. Once they recognized that time varies with the speed of the object, it became clear that one second of meson time was equal to nine seconds of earth time and that the mesons could easily get to the earth before they disintegrated. Once again, questioning an assumption resolved a seemingly irreconcilable situation.

It appears that just about every truly creative act reverses some basic assumption that is made about the situation under consideration. The most difficult aspect of this notion is that these assumptions are so fundamental, they are almost unconscious. It is difficult to see them, much less change them. In other words, in order to change your point of view about a situation, you have to have one to start with. If you are unaware of the viewpoint or set of assumptions you are taking, it's difficult to change it.

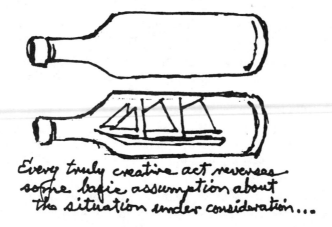

Every truly creative act reverses some basic assumption about the situation under consideration...

The following problem solving technique explores the basic assumptions in the problem, systematically reverses them, and offers new, potentially fruitful opportunities for resolution.

THE SCENARIO

The problem involved SBB Manufacturing, a large producer of non-woven materials such as clothing lining, automobile insulation, and hospital gowns. SBB identified a large market opportunity in supplying automobile repair shops with a new material for disposable shop rags — rags for cleaning and wiping oil and grease residue and spills.

The disposable rags replaced the re-usable shop rags supplied by industrial launderers; they recycled cloth rags by cleaning them and returning them to the shops each week. The cloth rags were often returned torn and worn, and occasionally they had embedded metal shivs capable of gouging man and machine.

SBB, on the other hand, offered clean, soft, strong rags. They had the feel of cloth and could be laundered, but they were less expensive for the mechanics. Another benefit was that each night they threw the SBB rags in the trash, instead of having to store the used cloth rags, which were full of oil, grease, and solvents, and created a fire hazard.

Everything was going well for SBB until the Environmental Protection Agency (EPA) created a new regulation. Suddenly, oil or grease soaked rags were considered hazardous materials, and companies were limited to the amount of hazardous materials they could dispose of each month. The amount of SBB contaminated rags that the large auto shops used far exceeded the 100 kilos per month that the EPA was allowing.

The auto shops had just five months to comply with the new EPA regulations, and they informed SBB that they would go back to cloth rags unless something could be done about the situation.

All of the ideas that SBB thought of either cost too much money or took too much time. As a result, we were invited by the marketing head to run a creative session to help SBB out of the mess.

OPENING

The first three questions of Assumption Reversal are fundamentally the same as initial questions for the previous two techniques and for Kaleidoscope. If you have used any of those processes for your problem, feel free to re-use the information where it is appropriate.

A. Describe The Problem

Write a brief (3-5 sentences) description of the problem.

SBB Manufacturing makes disposable shop rags for the auto repair industry. They replace re-usable cloth rags much like disposable diapers replaced diaper laundering services.

The EPA has passed a regulation that has declared oil soaked rags to be hazardous materials and has limited the disposability of these rags to 100 kilos per month, a figure which is easily exceeded by large shops. These shops have five months to comply with the regulation and have threatened to go back to the laundering service unless SBB can help them out of their predicament.

B. What Have You Tried?

What have you tried to resolve your situation, and why do you think that resolution has failed?

We considered having our sales people pick up the disposable rags each week and disposing of them in our own incinerators that are equipped with scrubbers. We thought about helping build a private incinerator for the auto shops. We also discussed laundering the rags ourselves, and we thought of seeking new markets for our rags where they would not be used with grease or oil and would not be deemed hazardous material and would not fall under the new law.

The first two ideas wouldn't work because the incremental cost we would have to incur would price us higher than the cloth rags, and we would lose the business anyway. The third idea didn't make much sense to us because it would turn us into an industrial laundry business. The last idea doesn't look promising because the material has been optimized for the auto industry, and the changes in marketing, manufacturing, and distribution would still cost at least 10 million dollars over two years.

C. List Other Obstacles

What other obstacles stand in the way of a successful solution?

The industrial launderers are already coming back to their old auto repair customers, reminding them that they have an alternative that is in compliance with the EPA regulations.

> At this point, it's important to understand that the industrial launderers did not have to contend with the EPA regulations because their heavy-duty washing operation diluted the contaminants sufficiently to allow them to be introduced into the municipal sewer system.

D. Summarize With A "How to. . ."

Summarize what needs to be changed in your situation in one sentence beginning with the words "How to. . . ."

How to maintain rag supplies to auto repair shops in a way that is cost effective.

REVERSAL

In this section, you look for fundamental assumptions about your problem, then turn them around.

A. List Five Assumptions

Sit back and think about your situation for a minute. You may even want to look through your description of the problem again. Try to find at least five fundamental assumptions that you are making about your situation.

These assumptions are so obvious that you take them for granted, they are so obvious that you never even consider them when you think about your problem.

1. The rags need to be disposed of.
2. Auto repair shops use the rags to absorb oil.
3. The industrial launderers are our competitors.
4. Auto repair shops use oil that is hazardous.
5. The EPA laws cannot be changed.

B. Reverse The Assumptions

Make a new list, called the reversal list, by taking each assumption and turning it around to its opposite.

1. The rags don't need to be disposed of. They may be kept by the repair shop.
2. The auto repair shops use the rags to absorb something other than oil.
3. The industrial launderers are our allies.
4. Auto repair shops use non-hazardous oil.
5. The EPA laws can be changed.

FINDING OPPORTUNITIES

A. Make Forced Relationship Forms

Develop a series of five Forced Relationship Forms. Over each Key Column, write each assumption reversal. Over each Insight Column, write your "How to. . ." statement.

B. Look For Insights

Force relationships between each reversed assumption and your "How to. . ." statement.

Rather than show all five Forced Relationship Forms, we will only show the one from which the final solution was developed.

(Key Column) Launderers are our allies	(Insight Column) How to maintain supplies to shops
We join forces with the launderies. We have something the laundry needs. We go on sales calls with the laundry.	1. Develop a laundering program for ourselves. 2. Let our sales force market laundry products. 3. Find a way to have laundries market our towels.
We buy laundry and put them out of business.	4. Find a way that the laundry can't comply with EPA either.
We put laundry facilities into auto shops. Laundry launders our rags.	5. Help auto shops with disposal problem. 6. Sell our rags to laundries.

C. Pick An Idea

Look through your ideas in the Insight Column of all five Forced Relationship Forms. Choose the best idea or ideas which move you toward your solution.

> If you don't like any of the ideas, you may look for other assumptions, reverse them, and follow the same steps. Or, you may want to look for another "How to. . ." statement.

Combine two ideas from above: Instead of retailing our towels to the auto shops, wholesale them to the laundries.

D. Dissect The Idea

Take your chosen idea and dissect it, looking for what is useful and what is missing.

Useful

1. The laundry supplies our towels to the auto shops and helps the shops comply with the EPA.
2. For the laundry, once they have purchased the towel, they can re-use it many times.
3. The work load for our salespeople is dramatically cut because they only have to sell to a relatively few wholesalers instead of many auto shops.

Missing

How to convince the laundry to market our products.

E. Develop Ideas

List as many ideas as you can think of to fill in what is missing in your solution.

Ideas

1. Purchase our own laundry which will be captive for our products.
2. Get the existing laundries to see value in marketing our products. Our rags are cheaper than theirs, but wear just as long. In addition, they are more absorbent.

Idea Chosen

We will pursue idea #2. If we can't get the laundry to see the merits of the idea, we will look to buy a competitive laundry service, leaving the existing management in place, and make our products the only ones for sale.

What was most significant about this solution was this: At the beginning of the session, it had been assumed that we had to develop a way to safely and economically transport or destroy the contaminated towels. SBB had spent millions developing the towel, and it was facing the possibility that they were useless.

The irony of the solution of changing the marketing strategy is that the rags were originally developed to replace the industrial business. Now, they are being sold to the laundries who are being more profitable, and SBB is making much more money than if they were selling them on a retail basis.

By the way, the key to the puzzle that opens this section is to reverse the assumption that the word "flies" is a verb and the word "time" is a noun. If you look at "flies" as a noun and "time" as a verb (as in timing a race), the answer comes easily. Look at it punctuated:

Time flies? Not I. They fly too fast.

A FINAL TECHNIQUE

It is possible that after having gone through all these techniques, your situation is still unresolved. If this happens, let another part of yourself, your sub-conscious, work on it by leaving it alone and doing something else. Let it cook for a while on your mental back burner, and return to it from time to time to see if any new insights have boiled up to the surface.

One way to help this slow-cooking process along is to vary your routine: take a different route home from work, change some pattern of behavior, some sequence that you normally follow, and let your sub-conscious be your guide.

A FINAL THOUGHT

We have been engaged in exercises that help us develop the discipline to step outside ourselves, and objectively observe what we are doing. When developed, this ability makes us more profoundly creative problem solvers by freeing us to adapt and change based on what we see.

This "self-watching" is a dynamic and exciting process, as we step in and out, diverge and converge. It is a process which is unique in the world. No machine or other living organism can take the place of your particular perceptions and your abilities to change them. Self-watching is one of those characteristics which make us fully human. Taking advantage of your ability to change your point of view, then, is claiming your creativity. Claim it now and you and your business will be richer for the experience.

Innovation, Inc.
— Group Style

Harnessing the
Creative Power of a Group

SOLVING PROBLEMS WITH GROUPS

M ost of this book has focused on the *individual* creative process because creativity is a highly personal experience. It involves being who you are and using your own particularly unique set of perspectives, values, ideas, and insights to solve important issues through your personal expression of these perspectives.

However, the reality of the world, and particularly of the business world, is that problems are not solved in a vacuum. Other people must be involved in your expression and the quality of *their* lives increased before your creative efforts are meaningful and can make a significant impact on our business and our clients/customers.

So we live with the paradox of maintaining our own fully human uniqueness, while confined and challenged by the group setting.

MAINTAIN YOUR UNIQUENESS
IN A GROUP SETTING

WHY BOTHER WITH GROUPS?

Individuals, not groups, create. Ideas are born in individuals, not in a collective group consciousness. While ideas are stimulated by group interaction, with one thought spawning the next in a well-run group, in the end, the idea coalesces in the mind of an individual. However, if handled sensitively and carefully, a group can greatly enhance the individual creative process.

The group setting affords at least five distinct advantages.

1. It Insures Buy-in And Commitment From The Participants.

The single best way to get someone to do what you would like them to do is to ask for their help. One of the finest compliments we pay others is soliciting and using their ideas. By finding value in the ideas of others, you are finding value in their private thoughts. You affirm the most unique and delicate parts of them in a more significant way than a pay raise, an ''atta boy,'' or some other form of acknowledgement.

When you sincerely solicit opinions from others, they tend to feel an integral part of your goal and will do what they can to insure success. They become willing participants in the implementation scheme; they become people who will fix something when it doesn't go the way it was planned, rather than saying "it was a good idea, but it just didn't work."

In Chapter Three's diaper facing problem, we strongly recommemded the plant's participation in the problem-solving session, even though it appeared to be R&D's problem. Their participation not only developed new perspectives of the situation, but by involving the plant, the ultimate implementability of the solution was insured. After all, the plant would eventually have to be part of the solution.

2. Group Problem Solving Builds Trust.

Another positive benefit of finding value in other's ideas is the relationship it builds. You automatically become a person to be valued and trusted if you are "smart enough" to see how good their ideas are. This trust allows group members to be more spontaneous and unreserved about thoughts that might otherwise have been judged inappropriate.

The trust factor helps to develop highly divergent thoughts, and the more divergent the ideas, the greater the chances that a truly wonderful notion will present itself. The atmosphere of group creativity promotes openness, and it helps people relax into sharing the more intimate details of their work, thereby raising understanding and appreciation.

3. It Aids The Personal Development Of The Participants.

The way you deal with ideas generated in the meeting serves as a powerful model for the other session participants. The more open and receptive you are to accepting other's ideas, the better your chances of finding innovative answers to your problems. The attitude is infectious and spreads easily through an organization. It helps others feel more willing to value the unusual and the challenging and creates a general improvement in interpersonal skills.

4. It Increases The Influence And Leverage Of The Solution.

As demonstrated in Chapters Four and Five, many people need to sign on to your solution willfully for it to be successful. Often these people work outside your area of influence, but they come on board because they know and respect another member of the problem solving group.

There is power in numbers. When a whole group agrees to a solution, the weight of numbers creates momentum more powerful than most individuals. Key decision makers feel more comfortable with solutions scrutinized by many points of view because chances are greater that more gaps have been filled.

5. A Group Setting Results In More Powerful Ideas.

Regardless of how good your idea is, the group can always help you improve it. Using the four creative skills, a group constructs more thorough, more carefully considered solutions than most individuals. But your ability to succeed with a group is determined ultimately by many factors involving your attitude, as well as the resources the group brings to the creative session.

This chapter is concerned with all the considerations necessary to insure that you will get that breakthrough idea from your group.

PROBLEMS AND PROCESS

There are two types of problems most appropriate for group problem solving: fixing something that doesn't work, and developing something new.

Fixing Something That Doesn't Work

You have a manufacturing process which fails to make acceptable product. Your sales incentive plan caused sales to drop. Your quality circles think they have nothing to talk about. Your pet twelve million dollar R&D project is about to dissolve because nobody can figure out how to commercialize it. You are losing accounts because you cannot service them efficiently.

There is no end to long-standing problems in business, problems which cost millions of dollars. Group sessions bring fresh points of view to these problems, creating new energy and synergy for their resolution. Solutions are only as far away as a new perspective, and groups present new opportunities and potential for that perspective to emerge.

Developing Something Totally New To Expand And/or Enhance Current Capabilities

What is the next product improvement? In what ways can we capitalize on our strong trademark to expand our product line? How can we meet the competition's latest invasion into our market? How can we take our current product and change it in a way that doubles its market? That triples it? How can we re-evaluate our mission and goals to bring more focus and purpose to our business?

Innovation is an infinite process. There is no point when you sit back and continue to ride on a job well done. Without the continuous application of energy, the company coasts. And everyone knows that coasting ends at a dead stop.

Group creative sessions can take what is, and look at it differently to make it unique, more effective, faster, cheaper, better. The collective energy and focus of a group can find new nuggets of opportunity in the oldest, most thoroughly developed product, service, or market.

What would you like to fix in your organization? What is the impossible problem that everyone has learned to live with? What's the most expensive dilemma you have? What do you have that you would most like to improve? What product or service would you most like to enhance? What is the mission of your group? Your company? What are your plans for realizing it?

The best, most creative answers to these questions can be discovered in your next group session. You may, and probably will, work on them individually, but the group can take you into areas you might never think to consider alone. It is like shopping for clothes with a friend who cajoles you into trying on a suit you would never otherwise have touched. But when you look in the mirror, you discover it is what you have been looking for all along.

It is difficult for us to understand that the problems for which there seem to be no solutions have an *unlimited* number of potential solutions. We simply need to see them. A good, positive, imaginative, well-run creative session affords the best opportunities for making them visible.

THE GROUP PROCESS

If this is the first time you are involved in a creative session, you might want to keep the process as simple as possible.

For example, define your problem with a series of "How to. . ." statements.

How to increase our budget by 25 percent to beef up our advertising budget
How to get the boss to increase the budget by 35 percent
How to find an extra $300,000 (25 percent) in our existing budget
How to steal an extra $300,000
How to get $300,000 worth of advertising for free
How to increase our sales by cheaper means other than advertising

And so on. . . .

Have the *decision maker* (discussed in detail later in this chapter) pick the most interesting "How to. . .," and begin the first divergent session by brainstorming ideas for that statement. Continue by having the decision maker choose the most interesting ideas, discuss what is useful, what is missing, and define a more specific "How to. . . ." The process repeats until a satisfactory solution path is developed.

This is a simple, straightforward approach that works for many problems, especially where the group has been prepped ahead of time and comes in armed with ideas.

If this fails to solve the decision maker's dilemma, you probably need a stronger process. Take a group through the Kaleidoscope model in Chapter Three.

When you are stuck, all the impossible problem techniques of Chapter Six are also applicable in groups. However, if you use the power of the group properly, and everyone is aware and pays attention to the roles and structures in the meeting, you will rarely, if ever, have to use those techniques. It is our experience that if the group is well cast, and if the pre-session homework is done with the decision maker, all we have to do is stand out of the way and direct traffic in our creative problem-solving sessions.

GETTING THE MOST POWERFUL IDEAS FROM THE SESSION
Casting

Many factors need to be considered in creating the group. We are often asked if there is a "magic number." There is — six to eight people. With less than six, you limit the variety of perceptions. With more than eight, participants do not have enough "airtime." Someone mentally retires from the group by not participating, disturbing a delicate interpersonal power balance. Can a session be run with more or less? Of course, we do it many times. Often it simply cannot be helped. But with more than eight or less than six, the potential increases that you will not get what you need because the group demands increasingly more skillful management, as well as more forceful and imaginative participants.

Given the fact that we have a numerical corridor that needs to be satisfied, what factors need to be considered in filling these slots?

First, attention needs to be paid to the organization as a political environment. Who are the power people that can influence whether or not your idea is implemented? Get at least one, if not more, into your creative session. Who would be the person most likely to block the implementation of your solution? If possible, get him or her into the group. It is difficult for people to be part of the problem and the solution at the same time.

Who would be the person most likely to block your solution?

On the other hand, don't take people who would be too recalcitrant. Without the aid of professional facilitation, this person might present too large an obstacle to overcome.

Second, find those people who will furnish the most divergent viewpoints. Recruit Analyzers, Implementors, Collaborators, and Imaginators. Represent each of the four areas for innovation. Get an accountant, a human resource person, a manufacturing representative, someone from graphics and design.

Fill the other slots with people who have knowledge, expertise, and/or vested interests that might be brought to bear on the problem.

You may also invite the person who is to be the ultimate recipient of your solution. For example, if you are developing a more efficient manufacturing system for the plant, involve one of the hourly machine operators in your session. If you are trying to develop a new dog food, invite a dog owner to the session. An end user provides a critical perspective which can not be duplicated by anyone else.

It is also important to invite people who think fluently and flexibly. By fluently, we mean the ability to generate many ideas on a given topic, and flexibly means the ability to develop different types or categories of ideas about a topic. You may want to consider the strange guy in research that nobody can quite understand, or the zany woman in marketing who is always working on ten different projects at once.

You might also consider taking a vertical slice of the organization. Find people who represent different levels of the hierarchy. The session will give junior people an opportunity to develop peer relationships with those normally outside their sphere of influence. At the same time, it will supply you with unique perspectives.

Finally, look for people with generally positive attitudes about the organization, perhaps those who are considered fast-trackers. These people have additional motivation to perform in a supportive and constructive way.

With idiots, naysayers, and boring people in your group, you are better off solving the problem alone. With a powerful, dynamic, and positive thinking group, the creative *potential* far exceeds what the individual can do alone.

Preparation

Like many things in life, preparation is 90 percent of the job. If the creative session is carefully and thoughtfully prepared, if all the elements are thoroughly considered and executed, it can't help but succeed. The difficult homework significantly reduces what's left to chance. In what follows, we will discuss the important elements to consider in the planning phase of the creative session.

Marketing The Session

Once the participants are selected, it is important they understand the value of the session, as well as the personal contribution you feel they can make to its success. If you can accomplish this in a way that is meaningful to them, they will arrive at the session with the appropriate attitudes.

The most important factor in developing these attitudes is your "neediness" for ideas from the group. If you have tried potential solutions and failed, if nothing you can think of works, and if the problem wakes you up at 3:00 a.m. in a cold sweat, you probably have the proper mind-set for a group session. The most successful sessions are those with the greatest need for solutions. You must be hungry for *any* idea that will take you where you need to go, independent of its source. You must be willing to listen to *anyone* with an interesting thought you can use. You should be thinking, "God, please, just give me an idea!"

To get the most from the creative session, it is best not to have a potential solution to the problem *firmly fixed* in your mind. If you have a potential solution and you want to use the group to test its efficacy, or if you want to see if they can come up with something better, then you want to have a different kind of meeting, not a creative session. Holding a creative session under those circumstances will waste both your time and the group's. You will simply lack sufficient motivation to be open and receptive to new points of view. And the group will know it — quickly — and shut down. So the first thing to do is to communicate with your potential participants individually and let them see your "hunger" and willingness to hear their ideas.

If you are going to send a memo about the session, address it individually. Don't make it part of a distribution. If you want to tell them who else is invited, include it in the body of the letter, or simply let them ask.

An individually addressed letter is special and important. So is your session. So are your participants. Communicate that significance. When inviting potential participants, consider their special strengths, skills, and expertise, and tell them why they would be valuable to the group.

Tell each invitee what their role in the session will be and what problem they are going to be working on. Ask them to bring ideas, even to solicit ideas from others, so they can walk into the session ready to rock and roll.

You might also send them any data or relevant information to help them generate ideas. If you can bring their attitude and thinking up to speed before the session, your probability of success goes up measurably.

Choose several possible dates to have the session and ask potential participants to indicate their availability on each of those dates.

Finally, make sure that you, not your secretary, follow up the memo in a few days with a phone call or get-together. There is no substitute for the personal touch. You want the group to understand that the session is very important, important enough to deserve your personal attention. Use your imagination to make your session as different and interesting as possible.

The Physical Environment

Many environmental factors contribute to the group's creative productivity. First, whenever possible hold your meeting away from the normal work environment. It is far easier to find new mental perspectives to a business problem if the physical perspective is different too. If possible, hold your meeting away from work, such as at a training center, a local hotel, or even at someone's home. Aside from the obvious benefit the change of venue affords, it is less likely the group will be interrupted, and it is more difficult for people to remain tied to the problems at the office when they are away.

If you cannot get away from the work environment, find an internal place in which there are no phones. (It's not enough to have a phone in the room that no one will answer when it rings.) Let a secretary know where everyone is, and have everyone in the meeting give their constituents back in the work place that secretary's number. When you take breaks, someone can check in with that secretary for messages.

Schedule breaks frequently enough that the meeting participants need not be out of touch for too long with some "crucial" piece of work that needs their attention.

This bring us to another point. Try not to go longer than one hour without taking a ten-minute break. This goes for all meetings, not just creative sessions.

At the beginning of any meeting the attention level is high. For many reasons, focus wanes as the meeting progresses. People get ideas that have nothing to do with the problem on the agenda, or someone in the meeting gets upset or annoyed with someone else. This distress is internalized, and the net result of withholding it is boredom and non-participation. And as the meeting progresses, even the most zealous group member gets tired and isn't as mentally sharp as he or she might be. So at the end of an hour, the bodies are in the meeting, but the minds are taking a trip. Frequent breaks allow bodies and minds to reunite, and group members return to the meeting intact and ready to work.

Third, the room should be large — the larger the better. A good rule of thumb is to use a room which comfortably accommodates three times the number of people you have in the session. People's freedom of thought seems to be directly related to the amount of physical space between them and their nearest neighbor.

Also, separate the people in the room. This cuts down on the side conversations and makes concentration easier. Open space also allows people to walk around while they think and talk. Many people need the kinesthetic stimulation walking affords. It helps them find new ideas and insights as well as keeps them fresher longer.

Room temperature is another factor in keeping them "fresher longer." Try keeping it on the cool side until someone complains. Warm rooms put people to sleep.

Have refreshments available in the room (coffee, fruit, juices, nuts, and cheese) so people can refuel themselves. The brain is the body's single largest energy consumer. Avoid or limit snacks with refined sugar if you can. Refined sugar takes the body through wide spans of high and low energies in short periods of time, and it can short circuit the thinking processes crucial to your imaginative session. For some people, caffeine can have the same effect.

Make sure the room has plenty of wall space for taping or tacking up sheets of newsprint with the group's ideas on them. People need the visual stimulation of the ideas as a constant, subliminal reminder to help them generate more and better ideas.

One way of arranging the seats for the meeting would be a semi-circle with the easel positioned on the mid-point of the diameter so that everyone can see it. If people need a table, then a round table eliminates power positions.

Additionally, make sure there are plenty of stands, easel pads, markers, pens, and masking tape to place the idea-filled sheets around the room.

If your meeting is off-site, choose a conference center over a hotel, if you have a choice. In general, conference centers are much better prepared than hotels to handle the needs of business meetings.

If the session is for a half-day, do it in the morning. If it is a whole day, make lunch light (salads are great). The old adage "a full stomach makes a dull mind" is true in creative sessions.

Finally, celebrate your brilliant success *after* the work is done with a cocktail party and a big dinner or another kind of upbeat affair. A sincere celebration is an important reward for work well done by people who have shared their thoughts and ideas.

ROLES AND STRUCTURES IN CREATIVE PROBLEM SOLVING MEETINGS

Creative meetings are most effective when there are three basic roles: the decision maker; ideators, or idea people; and a facilitator. The decision maker evaluates ideas and makes decisions based on them; ideators give ideas; and a facilitator runs the meeting.

Every creative meeting should be run in a series of two-part, diverging-converging episodes where the first episode allows the Kid in your thinking process to generate ideas freely, and the second episode uses the Judge to evaluate the ideas and make decisions about which notions to pursue further.

The second divergent episode is based on the evaluations made in the first convergent episode, the third divergent episode is based on the evaluations of the second converging phase, and so on until the problem is solved.

For example, in the initial diverging episode, the group might generate ideas about how to make a manufacturing operation more efficient. In the converging phase that follows, a decision might be made to concentrate on the raw materials preparation. The second divergent phase now develops ideas on raw materials preparation, and the second converging episode decides that what is missing in all of these ideas is that they cost too much in terms of capital expenditures.

The third diverging phase might generate ideas on how to minimize the capital expenditures involved in implementing these ideas, and so on. The challenges and problems revealed at the end of one converging stage are the starting point for the next diverging episode. The diverging/converging iterations stop when the problem is resolved and there are no more obvious roadblocks to implementation.

As always, the problems and issues that any converging episode ends with need to be phrased in the form of "How to. . ." statements. Each divergent phase should last from five to fifteen minutes, working with short bursts of energy. The converging phase is much harder and demands more time and thought.

The Decision Maker

One who blows the foam off his glass is not really thirsty.
— Talmud

The decision maker is the most important member of the group in the creative session, for it is he or she that ultimately chooses the ideas and pathways to solutions that will be implemented.

The decision maker should be the person with the greatest immediate personal stake in a successful resolution of the problem. Although, theoretically everyone stands to gain, somehow the decision maker has more to gain than others. It is the decision maker who implements whatever decisions are made in the meeting, and it is the decision maker who takes the blame if the solution doesn't work. The problem belongs to the decision maker.

Typically, in forward-looking organizations, the decision maker role moves down through the hierarchy the closer it comes to executing a strategy.

For example, as a chemical research director you might be a decision maker when it comes to developing new research directions for your group, but one of your managers might assume the decision maker role when it comes to fleshing out these directions with concrete programs. The chemist who reports to the manager might be the decision maker when it comes to developing pathways to execute these programs successfully, and finally the technician reporting to the chemist might become a decision maker in deciding how best to run the experiments.

This system creates a great sense of ownership in a company, a sense of personal investment difficult to duplicate even with raises and promotions.

In our experience, when the decision maker format is used, the person in the role of the decision maker must be willing to be the most creative person in the session. Why? Because we have defined creativity as both generating ideas and evaluating them. Since ideators only generate ideas, and the decision maker both generates and evaluates them, the decision maker is the most creative person in the room. In addition, only the decision maker integrates the perceptions of others into his or her thinking, another key element of the creative process.

This is why we feel the role of the decision maker is the most difficult in the group creative process. For most people, it is relatively easy to generate copious amounts of wild ideas, but the decision maker takes those ideas and turns them into viable implementable solutions within the constraints of time, technology, money, and people. And this is why it is so important for the decision maker to be hungry for ideas. Without the drive to find new perceptions, it will be very difficult to have a truly successful session. In fact, this is a lesson we learned by experience.

Last year, we were contacted by the marketing director of a new line of frozen food which had been in the market place for about two years. She felt she needed a creative session to help her develop ideas for an innovative merchandising campaign for a new product line. This was a campaign to convince grocery store managers to buy more product and stock it in a favorable location.

After an initial meeting with her, it became clear that whatever plan she developed would be implemented by her regional sales managers since they deal directly with the supermarket chains.

In our infinite wisdom, we suggested she make one of these sales managers the decision maker for the session. She contacted him, and he agreed.

A week later we held the session, and it was dismal. The group was lifeless. We used every technique in our repertoire, but nothing was interesting to our decision maker. Finally, as the session drew to a close, we asked him in exasperation what was going on.

He simply said, "But I don't have any problem pushing the new frozen product. The reason I don't do it is that I don't make as much money as I do when I promote our older, established line."

The sales person was not hungry for ideas because he did not own the problem, and as a result, the whole session was far less successful than it might have been.

The Decision Maker Diverges

The role of the decision maker alternates through the course of the meeting depending on whether the group is diverging or converging. In the divergent, brainstorming portion, there are only two roles: facilitator and ideators. The decision maker joins the ideators. In fact, he or she sets the example for the ideators by offering the kinds of ideas he or she is looking for.

During the convergent, evaluative phase, the decision maker resumes the role of evaluator. So the meeting alternates between two and three roles, depending upon whether the group is diverging or converging.

The decision maker *must* participate in the divergent phase of each segment. The better ideator the decision maker is, the more motivated the other group members will be, and the greater the opportunities for a productive and efficient session.

The Decision Maker Converges

At the end of the first divergent episode, the decision maker chooses the most intriguing ideas which he or she would like to see the group develop in the next divergent episode. The criteria for choosing an idea at this point is excitement. Choose it for further development by the group if you find it interesting, intriguing, or exciting in any way. You don't have to know how to make the idea happen. Purposefully avoid feasibility. You (and the group) will get to the practical decisions later in the process.

If ideas are being written down, simply star the exciting ideas with a red marker. If there are no interesting ideas for the decision maker, the group needs to understand what is lacking in the present ideas so that they can develop more ideas to fill the gap.

If there are intriguing ideas (and there usually are), the decision maker paints a word picture of what he or she sees in the idea — perhaps three or four sentences creating an image for the group, making the idea come alive. This description is like describing a movie to a blind person:

> I see the assembly line running at twice the speed because this idea would mean only half as many stations. And I see the workers getting involved in designing the system, perhaps in daily meetings right there on the line. . . .

Next, the decision maker describes what is useful about the idea, then what is missing in the idea in terms of a statement beginning with the words "How to. . . ."

After the decision maker finishes, the group looks for any other ideas the decision maker has not chosen that should be considered. Here, the group looks to protect the decision maker to make sure nothing of potential value is missed. This point is also when the decision maker begins some real creative work, finding value in someone else's ideas and points of view.

The Ideator

> One has to multiply thoughts to the point where there aren't enough policemen
> to control them.
>
> — Stanislaw Jerzy Lee

It is the ideator's job to give ideas — especially in the divergent phase of any session. And the ideas need not be confined to an area of expertise.

Ideators Diverge

Ideators are generalists during the divergent session, giving ideas from general knowledge and imagination, as well as their fields of personal expertise. The ideator uses the Kid, verbalizing all ideas which come to mind, independent of whether he thinks they are good or not. This description implies a willingness to open up, to expose yourself, to trust the process and the other group members — a willingness to express a novel, personal, or unpopular point of view just because it is different.

The ideator actually works for the decision maker, trying to respond flexibly and fluently to the "How to. . ." statements posed at the end of the last convergent sequence.

Ideators work best with legal pads, which allow them to jot down key words or phrases about an idea while waiting for an opportunity to speak. By writing the notion down, he or she can go on to develop another idea or build on former ones.

While giving a thought, ideators should resist describing, defending, or otherwise promoting it. There will be time for that in the convergent portion of the sequence. Any idea taking more than six to ten seconds to verbalize pulls the rest of the group members out of their own spontaneous process and forces them to pay attention to you, rather than their own mental connection with your idea. So get in and out quickly.

It is equally acceptable for an ideator to take a "mini-break" and drop out of the group to refine and play with your own thoughts or to get a cup of coffee, but don't pull anyone else out with you by involving them in conversations.

Many creative consultants talk about the need to defer judgment during the divergent phase of the process. In fact, this notion is the cornerstone of brainstorming, a technique that was introduced in the late 1920s by Walt Disney and expanded on by Alex Osborne in the mid-50s as a way for groups to generate ideas.

Brainstorming rules say that the value of an idea by itself is not important. More important are the concepts the idea triggers in its originator or in the minds of the other group members. The more ideas an individual or group can generate, the greater the chances of finding a good one. If individuals judge the rightness or wrongness of ideas, the flow of ideas closes down.

However, if the group understands that ideas will be evaluated later, they are better able to let go of these judgments. And this is where the principle of deferred judgment originates.

We don't totally subscribe to this theory. Ideators in creative sessions can not help having positive or negative reactions to the notions generated by the other group members. It is natural and a direct consequence of being engaged and involved in developing successful ideas for interesting and difficult problems. When forced to push this judgment away, they expend energy that might be better spent developing more ideas.

We don't want to waste that energy. Therefore, ideators should be encouraged to make judgments, but the kinds of dynamic judgments that are made by the Kid. If you like an idea, build on it by giving another idea. If you don't like an idea, consider what is wrong with it by developing "How to. . ." statements and respond to them by giving another idea. Instead of wasting time and energy fighting off judgment, use it to spur new ideas.

Record all your inappropriate thoughts and diversions on paper and use them to keep giving ideas in the session. Have fun! Wild ideas are often significant keys, and laughter can provide the lubrication to help reshape and rework them into something truly exciting.

Ideators Converge

After all the ideas have been developed, we go into the convergent or evaluation phase of the work, where the decision maker chooses those ideas that he/she thinks are worthy of further development. So the purpose of the convergent phase is to focus and prepare the problems for the next divergent episode. The ideator needs to keep thinking about ideas which respond to the decision maker's challenge and to note them as soon as possible on a legal pad.

The decision maker talks about the idea in which he has interest and then dissects it looking for what's useful about the idea and what's missing. The ideator then merely responds to the "How to. . ." questions.

After the decision maker has gone through all the ideas in which he/she has interest, it is the responsibility of the ideator to insure that there is nothing potentially exciting to the decision maker that might have been missed or overlooked in the evaluation.

The ideator considers this question: "Do I think this idea will be useful for the decision maker and help get him/her where he/she needs to go." They should not feel put out because his or her idea was not selected in the evaluation procedure.

For example, imagine the group has generated 30 ideas in the first divergent episode, and the decision maker has chosen numbers 2, 10, 15, 19 for further work. Your favorite idea is number 7. You feel it far outclasses any of the other ideas that are on the table (and coincidentally you are probably the one that gave it). Before proceeding further, ask yourself, "Will this really help the decision maker, or am I somehow prejudiced toward the idea?"

If your answer is that the idea will really help the decision maker, bring idea #7 to the decision maker's attention. Next, describe what you see in the idea without describing its value or defending its worth. It is the decision maker's responsibility to find worth or value in the idea. Your duty is to ensure that the decision maker understands the idea's content and intent.

Occasionally, an ideator develops a problem with some aspect of the meeting. He or she may not like the decision maker's choices, feeling that he or she had a solution in mind when they walked into the session. An ideator may have problems with the ideas that are being developed or just be frustrated with the process.

It is important that these problems surface and not be held in by the ideator. Keeping issues inside leads to apathy and disinterest, behavior which can eventually be fatal for the group. If there are such problems, the ideator must feel free to raise them, even if it stops the session. The input of every participant is critical, and the frustrated group member will work with decreasing efficiency until he or she is either out of the meeting altogether or the problem is solved.

Meetings often break down because there are too many problems on the floor at the same time. A group can only work effectively on one problem at a time. If someone in the group takes issue with the process, the decision maker, or any other aspect of the meeting, then two problems exist and the process must stop.

At this point, the person with the issue needs to make a decision. How serious is it? If the present decision maker agrees that it is also an issue for him or her, then the energy of the group can be redirected to the new, secondary problem, and the roles of ideator and decision maker remain the same.

However, if the issue is not shared by the decision maker, and if it is seriously inhibiting the ideator's thinking on the primary problem, then he or she can become the ad hoc decision maker around solving this secondary problem. The group then gives ideas and uses the process to resolve this issue. Once solved, then attention can return to the primary problem and the process continues.

In other words, in creative sessions, the problem shifts often, and sometimes the role of the decision maker shifts. But to stay productive, only one problem at a time with one decision maker can be on the floor.

Remember, ideators are in the session to work for the decision maker. . . and to have a good time!

The Facilitator

> *There are two ways of spreading light; to be the candle or the mirror that reflects it.*
> — Edith Wharton

The facilitator has perhaps the most complex and difficult work in the meeting. The facilitator concerns him- or herself with the structure and process of the meeting but stays out of the content. The facilitator neither gives ideas in the divergent section nor talks about ideas in the convergent phase. However, he/she is responsible for controlling everything else that happens in the meeting.

The facilitator, like the ideator, works for the decision maker, controlling the flow and attitudes and focusing the energy of the session. It is also the facilitator's responsibility to assure that the ideas get recorded properly in front of the group on flip charts as the meeting progresses.

A facilitator makes a group a team

Choosing A Facilitator

Choose the facilitator with these criteria.

- The facilitator must be a disinterested party with little at stake in the specific problem.
- The facilitator should understand the problem, however, and know what the decision maker wants to accomplish.
- Ideally, the facilitator should be on a peer level with the decision maker, not a low-level, recent hire from Human Resources.
- The facilitator needs to be interpersonally strong and have the ability to show warmth and empathy toward each member of the group.
- The facilitator is the guardian of the rules and regulations under which the meeting operates. He or she should be familiar with the roles of the other group members, as well as the problem solving model being used.
- The facilitator must be a cheerleader with the ability to energize the group, encourage and display humor, as well as be familiar with techniques to stimulate idea production at low points in the meeting.
- If the facilitator records ideas, he or she must write quickly and legibly, editing the long-winded ideas from the group into short bullet-point statements without changing or editorializing them.

Premeeting Planning

The facilitator must understand the problem, the dynamics of the group, and especially the personality of the decision maker. In the premeeting planning session, the facilitator learns what outcome the decision maker wants from the meeting and may be instrumental in casting the best ideators for the session. For the facilitator to control the meeting, there must be mutual rapport, trust, and respect with the decision maker. The facilitator should also have a say in the venue of the meeting. For off-site meetings, the conference center or hotel needs to meet the physical needs of the group. It is always a good idea to visit the facility ahead of time to make sure the material needs, room arrangements, snacks, meal planning, and all the other little details are understood and taken care of. There is enough to deal with in the meeting itself without having to worry about service or materials once the meeting has started. We often bring along an assistant who acts as a scribe for the session and serves as a liaison between the group and the facility.

Finally, if possible, the facilitator should contact each group member prior to the session to explain their roles, how the meeting is going to be run, and to respond to problems.

Starting The Session — Opening Moves

This is one of the most critical phases of the session. People need to get comfortable with each other and with the process. Interpersonal trust is crucial for forming the creative synergy possible in groups.

To make this happen, the facilitator loosens them up and helps them frame productive guidelines for interacting with the problem and each other. The guiding rule is that the group develops the rules and the facilitator assures that they are adhered to.

As we have said earlier, forced relationships is one of the single most powerful creative techniques, and it is with this tool that the facilitator can kill numerous birds with one stone. Using this technique, the facilitator can warm up the group, help them to set productive ground rules, and expose them to this technique which is so crucial to the process.

A. Introduce The People, Make Ground Rules.

Have each member of the group introduce himself in the following way:

1. Name and job.
2. Some personal accomplishment that they are proud of that no one else in the group is aware of. (This opens them up by revealing something about themselves in a positive way to the other group members.)
3. Name a ''creative hero'' — someone who they each individually admire and hold in high esteem for creativity (living or dead), and someone who is not associated in any way with the business or the problem at hand. It could even be someone fictional like Sherlock Holmes or Captain Kirk from *Star Trek*.
4. Then finally challenge them each to force a relationship between the unique attributes of their personal hero and one or two ground rules for the session to make it as creative and productive as possible.

Use all the ground rules that are generated in a way that is consonant with your understanding of what it takes as an ideator or decision maker to make the meeting work. You have made them comfortable, exercised their imaginations, and given them reference points to monitor their own behavior.

An alternative to the ''Creative Hero'' is to give them a list of famous quotes (see Appendix B). Ask them to find a quote with which they can particularly identify. Then have them force a relationship between the quotation and ground rules for having a creative and productive session. (You might use the creative hero as an idea generating technique later if the group needs a little extra stimulation.) The most important guideline for the facilitator is to resist giving the group ideas about anything. Use the group to help generate ideas which respond to their own questions, challenges, and concerns about what is going on.[1]

---

[1]The only exception to this rule is to suggest *ways* for them to generate additional ideas in any divergent segment. Never suggest the ideas themselves.

B. Introduce The Problem.

After the ground rules have been established, the decision maker describes the problem simply and briefly. And then answers questions for clarity only.

The group should ask open-ended questions rather than those which require a yes/no answer. Yes/no questions generally hide an idea about the problem or an idea for solving the problem. The time for those ideas is in the divergent section. Questions that start with who, what, when, where, why, how, explain, describe, say more about. . . are most appropriate.

The group should not spend more than 15 minutes in the questioning phase. The only person who needs to know totally what is going on is the decision maker. We want to familiarize the group with the problem, but in this case too much knowledge can be a dangerous thing for two reasons.

First, the bumblebees-can't-fly syndrome. If the group learns about all the blockages and frustrations and data that the decision maker has, they might make the same kinds of limiting assumptions, and so the chances are that their perceptions and ideas will be limited as well, and their value in the group process will be diminished.

Second, over-familiarization breeds negative attitudes. We don't want the group walking around in the morass of the present. Their time needs to be spent developing the positive energies of the future state, rather than feeling debilitated and overwhelmed with present conditions. A positive attitude contributes as much to the fluency and flexibility of their thinking as their intelligence and imagination.

The answers to the group's questions must be recorded and displayed on a wall at least through the initial phases of the meeting.[2]

C. Summary.

Finally, the facilitator checks in with the group, summarizing what has gone before and the steps that lie ahead.

It's like a final boarding call on a plane: "This is flight 40 to Reno, everybody comfortable with being here before the plane takes off?" Only now are you ready to proceed with the first divergent phase of the session.

The Facilitator And The Divergent Phase

To make the divergent phase productive, the facilitator pays attention to many different issues.

1. The Facilitator Keeps Everyone Focused On The Problem.

Gently remind people from time to time to refrain from side conversations. Tell the individuals that if they have ideas, comments, or anything that is

---

[2]The only data that you might not want to leave on display are the criteria for solution, which often limit initial ideas from the group.

not relevant for generating ideas for the problem on the floor, to write them on their note pads. Promise that there will be sufficient break times for socializing with the other group members.

The ideal divergent atmosphere is an uninterrupted flow of ideas, one right after another, with intensely focused excitement and energy. But often, someone has a question about an idea someone else gave. Either they didn't hear it, didn't understand it, or it referred to a part of the problem with which the ideator was unfamiliar. Almost instinctively, they blurt out a question, which someone else answers, and before you know it, no one is giving ideas. They are wrapped up in a discussion answering the ideator's question.

To move the group along, and to remain focused on the task of generating ideas, suggest that the group member make up an answer to the question, rather than stop the groups idea generation. It is less important to have a total understanding of the ideas in the divergent phase, as it is to be stimulated by the ideas to generate more. *Quantity in the divergent phase will get you quality in the convergent phase.*

2. The Facilitator Pays Attention To The Group's Energy.

Although there is a prescribed time period for each divergent session (10-15 minutes), if the group energy is low, take an early break. If the group energy is high, then keep going until that energy is played out, even if you go well beyond the 15 minutes. Use the group energy to maximize the productivity of the divergent activity.

It is also important to check periodically with members of the group who take longer than three or four minutes to give an idea. Kindly remind them how important their ideas are. If one person sits around without giving ideas, soon the group starts wondering what is going on. This gives the silent person too much power because the group's concentration is on that individual and not on the problem. Then the group's energy and enthusiasm starts to wane.

This is an important point about any meeting. How often have you seen someone remain silent through a meeting? Then, after everyone else has played their cards, Mr. Silent says something like "I've been listening to what everyone has been saying and this is what I think. . . ." The last to speak has the benefit of all that has preceded, and as the role of the summarizer, derives greater power within the meeting.

Often, bosses go into meetings and withhold their opinions for fear of influencing the meeting. However, that stance more often tends to inhibit the group, because they are all wondering where he or she stands. The wise manager divulges opinions upfront, then encourages staff to debate issues positively and creatively when opinions differ. Some managers disagree with this notion. They find it threatening. It is threatening — to the insecure. But the manager who rewards only those who agree can never trust advice and information coming from staff, diluting their usefulness and productivity.

3. The Facilitator Keeps The Ideas Flowing.

The facilitator arrives at the meeting armed with idea-producing techniques if the group seems to be lacking the ability to be fluent with ideas. The following is a list of suggestions that help to keep ideas flowing during a drought.

A. Do nothing. Silence is not necessarily an indication of a lack of ideas. Avoid jumping into the breech too quickly. Sometimes people simply need thinking time, especially if the last idea or problem was provocative. Let them try to work out of their own silence. After a while, you will be able to identify the differences between mental dullness and internal excitement.

B. Take a break.

C. Check with the group. Ask them if they are having trouble generating ideas or whether they just need time to incubate and sort things out.

D. Use the four basic types of manipulations. Ask groups to make something larger, smaller, rearrange it, or look at it from a different point of view. Have them do this with the ideas that have already been generated, as well as with things in the environment where the problem is occurring.

E. Use the introductions. Have the group think about their creative heroes. Tell them to have internal dialogues with these heroes and ask them for the ideas that their heroes might offer to the group if they were actually sitting in the session.

F. Ask the group to consider the fundamental assumptions they are making about the problem, and try reversing them as a stimulus for developing more ideas.

G. Ask the group to take a mental walk, find something personally interesting in the meeting environment and force relationships between these and more ideas to respond to the "How to. . ." statement.

H. Ask the group to think about how they would insure that the problem remain unsolved, or worsen, then use the reverse of these for more ideas.

I. Ask the group to change the verb in some of the ideas already developed.

J. Ask the group members if *they* can suggest ways for the group to develop more ideas. Whenever you run into difficulty, you always have the group there to help you.

4. The Facilitator Ensures All Thoughts Are Recorded.

RECORD ALL THOUGHTS

As ideas are being developed, the facilitator ensures that they are quickly, clearly, and concisely written on newsprint. The facilitator writes alone or uses a scribe. If ideas flow particularly quickly, both may have to write to keep the pipeline from backing up. Ideally, no one should have to wait for the recorder to finish to give an idea.

Remind the group that if their idea is not captured immediately then they should write it down themselves on their pads and then continue to develop ideas. As ideas are written on the newsprint, the facilitator should repeat that idea out loud, assuring the ideator that the idea has been captured. This frees them to generate more ideas.

The Facilitator And The Convergent Phase

Here the facilitator pays attention to the interaction between the decision maker and the ideators, ensuring that everyone in the group is clear about what is expected of them, and that everyone gets sufficient air-time for their views. The facilitator pays particular attention to the energy of the decision maker. It is tiring to understand, appreciate, and integrate five to ten perceptions which aren't your own. Remember, initially these ideas are not particularly exciting to the decision maker, so the work can be arduous. Be extremely supportive to the decision maker in the convergent phase. Empathize. Show that you understand and appreciate the difficulty of the job.

If the decision maker's energy begins to flag, take a break. Sometimes physical activity like deep breathing, stretching, or rubbing each other's shoulders helps. Recess for a short game of volleyball to re-energize the group. Fifteen minutes of intense physical activity works wonders for a low-energy group and a tired decision maker. Sensing group energy and creatively responding to its needs are two of the facilitator's most important functions.

Ideators also need care in the convergent section. Be sure they are clear about the decision maker's criteria for choosing ideas.

Often ideators require encouragement to raise issues the decision maker misses. In our experience, it is that one other point of view, coaxed from a reticent ideator, that provides the breakthrough. Recognize when people have something to say and are not saying it. Notice their gestures, their body language. Are they trying to catch your eye? Are they leaning forward in their chair? The other, more difficult symptom to recognize is withdrawal. People who have an idea but don't believe it will be taken seriously, often give up. They sit back in their chairs, with looks of defeat or disdain. Sometimes they will whisper their thought to a sympathetic neighbor. Don't let them get away. Challenge them to say what is on their mind. Then challenge the decision maker to understand, find value, and integrate. The group must understand that they cheat the decision maker when they see a way to help and don't speak up.

Work to keep the ideators engaged. When the decision maker chooses ideas, don't let the ideators sit around waiting. Have them watch the selection process, looking for the notions the decision maker misses. Keep them thinking and working. Encourage them to use their pads to work out new thoughts. Don't lose any opportunity to find yet another idea.

Remember, the ideators exist to help the decision maker to solve the problem. The environment is totally supportive and non-competitive. When the decision maker wins, everybody wins. When every person in the group feels free to express his or her point of view, and when the decision maker demonstrates a sincere hunger for additional perspectives, the group cannot fail.

DEVELOPING IDEA OWNERSHIP

The decision maker strives to develop ownership of the ideas generated that are not his or her own, to make a personal connection with them. It isn't until the decision maker fully grasps a notion and integrates it and all its implications into his or her thinking, that the idea stands a chance of being fully implemented.

If you are the decision maker, how do you go about gaining ownership? To own an idea, three things need to happen:

- You need to understand the idea — a challenge in its own right.

- Once you understand it, you need to appreciate it, to look at it as the Angel's Advocate, and try to find all the benefit the idea holds for you.
- And finally, you need to identify what's missing for you, what's keeping you from putting the idea in your bag of potential solutions and, with help from the group, bridge that gap.

Following is a step-by-step scenario describing the techniques for integrating ideas.

Understanding

Any idea or thought is actually composed of two parts: the content and the intent. In an idea, the content embodies the literal meaning of the words while the intent embodies the general principles behind the thought. It is very possible to understand the content of an idea but completely miss the point because the intent was missed altogether. We tell a story that clearly illustrates this.

Driving through a small midwestern town, a man stops at a gas station and asks the attendant to fill the car with gas. While filling the car, the attendant happens to look in the back seat and sees two large penguins sitting there. Visibly upset, the attendant approaches the driver and says, "You know, we have an ordinance in this town, and while you're here, you've got to take those penguins to the zoo." The man agrees amiably and drives off.

Three days later, as luck would have it, the man finds himself back at the same filling station asking the attendant again to fill his car with gas. The attendant looks in the back seat again and sees the same penguins, but this time they are wearing sunglasses and sandals. Angrily, he approaches the driver and says, "I thought I told you that you had to take them to the zoo while you were here."

The driver replies, "I did take them to the zoo; they loved it! Now they want to go to the beach!"

In this silly situation, the driver clearly understood the content of the idea — take the penguins to the zoo. But he missed the intent completely — lock the birds up.

The same misunderstanding, although perhaps more subtle in the office, is common in business. If you really need to communicate with someone, both elements of the communication, the content and the intent, must be clearly understood.

With this as background, try the following process to gain certain understanding of an idea which was not yours to begin with.

1. The person who thought of the idea paints a word picture of what the idea means in three or four sentences.

> Again, it's important that the ideator not defend the idea or talk about why it might be useful to the decision maker. It is the decision maker's job to find value in the idea. The decision maker tries to develop ownership or a connection with the ideas while ideators break connection with the ideas. These connections must be broken to free ideators to give more ideas.

2. The decision maker develops an in-depth understanding of both the content and the intent of the idea.

Understanding Content

One of the best ways of ensuring content understanding is for the decision maker to paraphrase the idea that the ideator has just explained. To begin the process of integration for the decision maker, talk about *the* idea rather than *your* idea or Joe's idea. It depersonalizes the notion and helps break the connection between the ideator and the idea. It shows the decision maker interacting with the idea alone, rather than with the source of the idea. And if eventually the idea gets rejected, the person giving the idea does not get rejected with it.

So the decision maker repeats the notion, starting with the words "The idea is . . .," reflecting an understanding of the words. If the paraphrase is accurate for the ideator, the content is clear. If not, the ideator repeats the idea, pointing out what was omitted or misstated. The decision maker paraphrases again, until the ideator confirms an understanding.

Understanding Intent

People do two basic types of thinking and problem solving, using both words and pictures. Words most accurately represent the content, but intent is in the domain of pictures. To ensure a full understanding of someone else's point of view, it is important to share the same words and the same pictures.

Often the pictures associated with a notion are buried in the pre-conscious. These pictures, when brought to the surface, tell a whole new story about the idea. The quality of the images expressed in an idea depends on how the idea is expressed. Be specific and concrete.

For example, here are two ideas:

- "Let's hold this meeting somewhere else."
- "Let's hold this meeting on the moon."

Even though both of these ideas are verbal, the second carries a stronger mental image because it is more specific. People get internal images through sensory information — smells, tasks, sounds, movement. The more specific the idea, i.e., the more sensory information it contains, the greater the chance it evokes pictures. You know what it would feel like in a reduced gravity environment like the moon; you have seen pictures of the moon; you have a sense of what it would sound like to communicate through space suits. So you get a picture.

One of the most powerful ways of developing these specific word pictures is to find an analogy or a metaphor that expresses your understanding of the intent of the idea in a different context, like illustrations in a book highlighting the text. To understand the picture portion of the ideator's notion, this is precisely what the decision maker needs to do.

So, after the decision maker and the ideator agree on the words, the decision maker finds an analogy that expresses his or her understanding of the idea. (Use the list of parallel worlds in Appendix D if you need some help.) Next, the ideator looks at the decision maker's analogy, and either accepts it or changes it by changing something in the analogy (*not* by changing the analogy itself). The ideator modifies the decision maker's analogy just as the decision maker paraphrases the ideator's words. The decision maker offers the analogy, not the ideator, because if the decision maker conceives the picture even if it is eventually modified by the ideator, there is a greater chance of him finding value in the idea.

It also shows the group how actively he is trying to gain a different point of view, helping to maintain the delicate power balance needed for the group to be effective.

If the ideator modifies the analogy, the decision maker finally shows understanding of the modified analogy by paraphrase.

Finally, having agreed on both the content and the intent, the decision maker finds value in the idea, expresses what, if anything, is missing from the idea, preventing it from being one he or she wants to explore further, and the group tries to help him fill that gap. If they can, the idea (or its modification) is brought forward with the rest of the ideas the decision maker has chosen. If they can't, the idea is dropped.

Following is a summary of the interaction we have just described using a specific example.

Suppose the problem on the table is how to decrease the time it takes to get preliminary market research data about a new product idea involving shaving cream that also deep cleans the face. One of the ideas that the decision maker has not chosen is to use in-house personnel for a preliminary investigation. But one of the ideators thinks it is important to consider.

1. The ideator offers the idea for consideration to the decision maker and expands on it, trying to paint a picture of what he sees.	1. Id: "I'd like you to consider using in-house personnel. What I see there is that we would give samples to employees. They would use it in the washroom, and after using it would report back to us."
2. The decision maker paraphrases the idea.	2. DM: "The idea is to use employees to do the initial concept screening."
3. The ideator accepts or changes it.	3. Id: "Yeah, that's right."
4. Decision maker now finds an analogy.	4. DM: "It's like giving a speech in front of my family before giving it in front of my Rotary Club."
5. Ideator accepts or changes it.	5. Id: "No, it's like putting your family on the same type of financial budget you put your Rotary Club on so they can actually experience it in the same way."
6. Decision maker agrees for understanding and does the final paraphrase.	6. DM: "OK, I see the difference. It's not an academic exercise then as much as a hands-on experience."
7. The decision maker now becomes the angel's advocate, finding value.	7. DM: "What's useful to me about the idea is that (A) it certainly would get results back quickly; (B) it would also help to keep the idea confidential by only using in-house consumers; (C) and it would make our employees more motivated by keeping them better informed about what we're doing."
8. The decision maker now makes his "How to. . ." statements.	8. "What's missing for me is how to elimate the positive bias that in-house employees would have about the idea since they have a vested interest in seeing it work."
9. The group develops ideas for bridging the DM's gap. (Remember, the DM now becomes an ideator.)	9. (A) Only choose employees who know nothing about what we're doing. (B) Choose relatives of employees who live in the same house as they do.
10. The decision maker finally accepts or rejects the notion.	10. "Yes, using in-house relatives would certainly make it acceptable because it solves my problem, and it includes the other things that I value. Let's include it in the next divergent phase."

This may seem like a lengthy process, and it certainly is not something you would use for talking with your neighbor over the back fence. However, when the need to communicate ideas is critical, such as when you desperately need new points of view for a pressing business problem, the process will help you make sure you don't miss an opportunity. Those who are the hungriest for a new idea will find integrating this process very easy.

Although the group creative session depends on the full, creative participation of all members to be completely successful, the session actually hinges on the decision maker. The success of this role depends on openness, receptivity, and on a willingness to evaluate and understand all ideas which appear in the session. The decision maker must be playful, spontaneous, very anxious to solve the problem, and very grateful to others for sharing their ideas. He or she must also be selfish, not taking ideas just to make an ideator feel better or for political reasons, but for the possibility that the idea may actually lead to a solution. If the decision maker embraces these attitudes and communicates them to the group, solutions will appear.

Next Steps After the Session

You have gotten an exciting solution, or perhaps two or three potential solutions, out of the session, and you have removed all of the apparent roadblocks by using the "How to. . ." statement. It is time to ensure success.

First, take your solution through Chapters Four and Five (Selling Your Solutions and Fool Proof Implementation) before you take the next step. Do it right away.

Then, if you are the decision maker, show the group in a creative way how much you appreciate the time, energy, and imagination they put into helping to resolve a knotty problem.

Have A Party

Throw a cocktail party and dinner for them, sometime after the session, where you acknowledge what you have done so far and any roadblocks you have encountered.

Write A Letter

Write a letter to their bosses expressing the unique contribution each individual has made to the success of the session. Copy the participants and the personnel department. Remember, make each letter different because each individual made a different contribution.

Give A Keepsake

Send them each a remembrance of the session with some metaphorical representation of your final breakthrough idea. When we worked with our group in Chapter Three, the decision maker sent to Lake Placid for mementoes of the 1980 Olympic hockey team. He received special pins which he distributed to each participant along with a letter of thanks.

Whatever you do, keep the group informed about what it is you are doing, and ask for their help if you run up against unforeseen problems. Let the group see the fruits of their labor, and make them proud of it. Share its success, and ensure their participation in the next creative session.

Summary

Meetings can be the single biggest time wasters and producers of negative energies in American business today. Most often, their purpose is not to solve problems but to exchange information which could be more efficiently distributed another way, to give strokes, or to rubber stamp a decision that has already been made. They are a waste of resources.

The vast majority of meetings should be used for problem solving. Meetings are the only places that bring together in one place the combined experiences, thoughts, and unique perceptions of informed people. To fail to use these mental libraries to solve problems is a squandered opportunity.

How often have you walked into a meeting, been given a handout of some sort, and after about 43 seconds been asked for penetrating insight into the information you have had so long to consider? If the information is important, and if ideas, potential problems, roadblocks, and considered analysis are being requested, pass out the information well ahead of time. Then ask people to bring their insights into the meeting.

If you need buy-in for a decision, give the decision ahead of time, then bring people together to do the required problem solving to resolve any potential negative consequences.

Most decision makers in business find this proposal threatening. Knowledge is power. If I give away important information before a meeting, in a way I'm weakening my position. If I keep the information to myself until the meeting, I maintain control over any objections or difficulties that may surface in the meeting because I have had a chance to think about the consequences and meaning of my data, and the others have not.

Unfortunately, this popular thinking leads to mediocre decisions and de-motivated employees. The only willing supporters of your point of view in the meeting will be those who favor political expediency as prime motivators for their professional careers.

On the other hand, independent thinkers (an endangered species in today's large businesses) will either say nothing, or act recalcitrant and look for negatives when you most need them to be the angel's advocate. Unfortunately, it is the independent thinkers who can best help you modify your decision to make it more powerful, and discover the hidden roadblocks and obstacles.

How do you change their attitudes? Simply give them data and time to consider it before asking their opinion.

Make sure your meeting has a facilitator who runs the meeting and who stays out of the content. Declare your position on the decision or information up front. Make yourself vulnerable. Invite the group to evaluate the decision creatively. Modify the idea with the Dissecting Ideas technique explained in Chapter Two which we used again and again in all the chapters of this book.

Consider dividing a large sheet of paper into three columns lengthwise with the following headings:

What's Useful About the Decision or Plan?	What's Missing in the Plan? "How to. . ."	Modifications of the Plan to Respond to "How to. . ."

Ask the group to diverge in all three columns. You will be surprised at how much more powerful your final solution and implementation will be, and how much more invested and willing your people will act.

The magic group numbers are six to eight. If you have a large number in the meeting, have them work in small groups, then report back to the larger session. The strength behind this type of approach is enormous.

Remember, those who are worried about losing power never really have it in the first place. You are not that small that you need to be that big.

Checklist for a Group Problem Solving Session

I.   Consider the type of problem
   A. Fixing something broken or creating something new. Both need to resolve an important problem.
   B. Do I already have an idea of what the solution should be?
   C. Is the issue highly specific?

II.   Casting
   A. The ideal number — 6-8 participants.
   B. Consider all the politics involved.
   C. Have people representing all four faces of creativity.
   D. All participants fluent and flexible thinkers.
   E. All participants with positive attitudes.

III.   Marketing the Session
   A. Communicate a sense of urgency and a hunger for ideas.
   B. Communicate personally with the individual participants.
   C. Provide a choice of dates for maximum participation.

IV.   Environment
   A. Off-site if at all possible.
   B. Room for a group three times this size.
   C. Physical comfort.

1. Frequent scheduled breaks.
2. Appropriate snacks provided.
3. Know how to control room temperature.
4. Is there adequate wall space?
5. Have plenty of flip chart stands, paper, tape, and marking pens for recording ideas and taping them to the walls.
6. Provide for lunch.

V. Roles and Structures

A. The Decision Maker
1. Has power and authority to make decisions, and to develop resources for implementing them.
2. Models ideator behavior in divergent phase.
3. Behaves as most creative person in group, integrating perceptions and developing ownership around ideas that were foreign before session took place.
4. Knows how to paraphrase and find analogies for ideators' suggestions.
5. Plays the role of the Angel's Advocate.

B. The Ideators
1. Strong, independent thinkers.
2. Excitement about participation.
3. Willingness to create and play by ground rules.
4. Strong need to help decision maker.

C. The Facilitator
1. Involved in process only.
2. Respected by group members in both formal and informal hierarchy.
3. Strong interpersonal skills.
4. Knowledge of process to be used.
5. Knowledge of idea-stimulating techniques.
6. Understanding of group dynamics and group process.

VI. Post Session

A. Have a celebration.
B. Letter of acknowledgement to bosses stating personal, unique contribution of each participant.
C. A keepsake of the session.

To Be Creative is a Choice You Can Make

Creative thinking is much more than a tool. It is more than a technique or collection of techniques, and it is more than a system for thinking differently. Creative thinking is a way of living your life.

If you have just worked your way through this book, it may all seem overwhelming. "Is a good idea worth all this work," you may be thinking? First of all, the answer is yes. With a process for creating high-value ideas or for solving high-value problems, it is relatively little work for such potentially high return.

Second, the more you do it, the less work it seems. When these concepts integrate themselves into your habitual thinking patterns, they become second nature. You think this way without thinking. It isn't work, it's normal. People who you now consider creative probably have incorporated many of these processes, or at least elements of these processes, into their thinking.

True creative thinking is infinite. There is no end to it. And hopefully, this may have been the beginning of it for you. Once you understand how to think creatively, you don't pull it out, use it to make something, then put it away. It's continuous. When you create your solution, you use your creativity to sell it (like 3M's Arthur Fry), and you use your creativity to implement it. Soon you find yourself constantly looking for opportunities, coming across discoveries when you least expect them, being visited by solutions to your most pressing problems.

Once again, here are the eight principles standing behind all that you have read:

1. Everyone is creative.
2. Creativity reduces risk.
3. There are four faces of creativity.
4. One does not live by data alone.
5. One picture is worth *more* than a thousand words.
6. There are no impossible dreams or problems (only limited dreamers and problem solvers).
7. The subconscious is a full partner in the creative process.
8. Creative thinking creates win/win situations (without compromise).

Now that you have finished the book, how do you feel about these principles? Do you see them as true for yourself? If not, what is missing? Using these and any others you think important, make your own set of principles. Write them down where you can see them, and they will remind you of your creative potential.

Finally, look at your "bookmark," the paper on which you wrote ideas for getting the most from this book in Chapter One. Allow yourself to sit back and reflect on the experience of the book, the ideas and concepts in it, and the notions you jotted down on the bookmark as you read through. Just let them sink in. Now that you have finished it, what final thoughts can you write down? With the benefit of hindsight, what secrets or insights do you have about getting value from this book that you didn't have when you began? If you have a friend who is reading the book, share your bookmarks with each other. You will be surprised at how different they are.

To be creative is a choice you can make.

If you take away nothing more than this understanding, you have taken something very powerful. Time after time we hear people say, "I surprised myself, I never considered myself particularly creative." Surprise yourself. Empower yourself. Take responsibility. Take all that you have learned back to your business and use it to create and implement relentlessly. Turn your business into Innovation, Inc. and it will be very successful. Make the choice to be creative, and in just that one step you will have traveled over half the distance to a new life.

Additional Skill Building (Chapter Two)

DIVERGENT THINKING

In the next ten minutes, list all the ways you can think for improving the washroom in your business or office. Please complete the exercise before reading further.

Generate at least 35 ideas in 10 minutes for improving a meeting room. (First describe a meeting room using a list of words or short phrases, then change your descriptions using the four basic types of manipulations:

- Making it larger, greater, or extending it.
- Making it smaller, deleting it, or miniaturizing it.
- Rearranging it, or adapting it, transposing it, substituting it.
- Considering it from a different point of view.)

Think of an object in your business you would like to improve. Come up with 50 different ideas for making it better. Record the time it took.

FORCING RELATIONSHIPS

Consider the task of replacing a valuable employee who has left your organization (Insight Column). Develop at least ten ideas/suggestions for how to do this by finding relationships or connections between finding a replacement and planning a successful party (Key Column).

Develop 10 different ideas for relating better with an associate with whom you have had past difficulty (Insight Column) by forcing relationships between the way you relate to the associate and doing a safety check on your car before making a long trip (Key Column).

Remember, in the characteristic column, explore the details, the actual mechanisms by which it works or happens.

FOR BECOMING THE ANGEL'S ADVOCATE

In 10 minutes, find as many things useful as you can with the following idea:

TO REDUCE OVERHEAD, BUSINESS PEOPLE SHOULD NOT BE ALLOWED TO TAKE VACATIONS.

In 10 minutes, using the forced relationship form, find as many things useful about the following idea as you can:

FOR BETTER WORKING RELATIONSHIP, THE BOARD OF DIRECTORS SHOULD WEAR MICKEY MOUSE EARS TO THEIR MEETINGS.

In 15 minutes, find as many valuable notions as you can using the forced relationship exercise for the following idea:

PEOPLE SHOULD GET MILD ELECTRIC SHOCKS IF THEY DON'T GET TO WORK ON TIME.

FOR DISSECTING IDEAS

Try finding ways to improve your productivity. Starting with the idea of using a squirrel to do some of your tasks, use forced relationships and idea dissecting techniques to find at least one opportunity that you can implement next week at no additional cost. Give yourself at least 30 minutes to work on this exercise.

See if you can diagram in 15 minutes the thought process that our acquaintance at the Chicago airport might have gone through using the idea dissecting technique. (Page 30)

Consider this problem:

HOW TO BECOME A MORE CREATIVE MANAGER

1. Develop at least 10 additional "How to. . ." statements by changing the verb in the statement.
2. Picking your favorite, see if you can get ideas for it by using either the dissecting technique or forced relationships.

Great Minds Inventory (Quotations)

ANALYZER QUOTATIONS

1. *He who has butter on his head should not walk in the sun.*
   — Talmud

2. *He who has imagination without learning has wings but no feet.*
   — Toubert

3. *Be sure of it, give me the ocular proof.*
   — Shakespeare

4. *One should not confuse the painter, the painting, and the easel.*
   — Bhagavad Gita

5. *Things are seldom what they seem, skim milk masquerades as cream.*
   — Gilbert

6. *One coin in a bottle rattles; the bottle filled with coins makes no sound.*
   — Talmud

7. *Grace is given of God, but knowledge is bought in the market.*
   — H.H. Clough

8. *God made integers, all else is the work of man.*
   — L. Kronecker

9. *Heat cannot of itself pass from a colder to a hotter body.*
   — R. J. E. Clausius

10. *Never try to teach a pig how to sing. It wastes your time and annoys the pig.*
    — Anonymous

11. *In baiting a mousetrap with cheese, always leave room for the mouse.*
    — H. H. Munro

12. *Don't hitch a horse and an ox to the same wagon.*
    — Talmud

13. *When you are an anvil, hold you still, when you are a hammer strike your fill.*
    — G. Herbert

14. *The weakest fruit drops easiest to the ground.*
    — Shakespeare

15. *The lion and the calf shall lie down together, but the calf won't get much sleep.*
    — Woody Allen

IMPLEMENTOR QUOTATIONS

1. *Going to bed with a woman never hurt a ballplayer. It's staying up all night looking for them that does you in.*
   — C. Stengel

2. *The most difficult part of getting to the top of the ladder is getting through the crowd at the bottom.*
   — A. Word

3. *Can the blind lead the blind? Shall they both not fall into the ditch?*
   — Bible

4. *Handle your tools without mittens, remember that the cat in gloves catches no mice.*
   — Ben Franklin

5. *The question "who ought to be boss" is like asking who ought to be the tenor in the quartet. Obviously, the man who sings tenor.*
   — Henry Ford

6. *The finest edge is made by the blunt whetstone.*
   — J. Lyly

7. *In skating over thin ice, our safety is in our speed.*
   — Emerson

8. *My guiding star always is, get hold of portable property.*
   — Dickens

9. *When in doubt, win the trick.*
   — E. Hoyle

10. *Knowledge may give weight, but accomplishments give luster, and many more people see than weigh.*
    — Chesterfield

11. *The wisdom of life is to keep on planting for the sown seed goes on growing whether we remember it or not.*
    — Henry Ford

12. *Not only strike while the iron is hot, but make it hot by striking.*
    — O. Cromwell

13. *Woe to him who makes a door before he has a house or builds a gate and has no yard.*
    — Talmud

14. *The man who blows the foam off his glass is not really thirsty.*
    — Talmud

15. *Have a care where there is more sail than ballast.*
    — Wm. Penn

COLLABORATOR QUOTATIONS

1. *There are two ways to spread the light, to be the candle or the mirror that reflects it.*
   — E. Wharton

2. *If you have two loaves of bread, sell one and buy a hyacinth.*
   — Persian saying

3. *If you put a chain around the neck of a slave, the other end fastens around your own.*
   — Emerson

4. *If nobody had ever learned to undress, very few people would be in love.*
   — D. Parker

5. *Does the eagle know what is in the pit? Or wilt thou go ask the mole.*
   — Wm. Blake

6. *The battle of Waterloo was won on the playing fields of Eton.*
   — Duke of Wellington

7. *The fire which seems extinguished often slumbers beneath the ashes.*
   — P. Corneille

8. *If two logs are dry and one is wet, the kindling of the two will kindle the wet one too.*
   — Talmud

9. *When the lion fawns upon the lamb, the lamb will never cease to follow him.*
   — Shakespeare

10. *A round man cannot be expected to fit in a square hole right away. He must have time to modify his shape.*
    — Mark Twain

11. *There is no excellent beauty that hath not some strangeness in the proportion.*
    — F. Bacon

12. *Laws are like cobwebs which may catch small flies, but let wasps and hornets through.*
    — J. Swift

13. *Your pain is the breaking of the shield that encloses your understanding.*
    — K. Gibran

14. *There is a banyan tree which has its roots upward and its branches down.*
    — Bhagavad-Gita

15. *Personal beauty is a greater recommendation than any letter of reference.*
    — Aristotle

IMAGINATOR QUOTATIONS

1. *Ruling a big country is like cooking small fish.*
   — Lao Tsu

2. *What is a weed? A plant whose virtues have not been discovered.*
   — Emerson

3. *Where the telescope ends, the microscope begins. Which of the two has the grander view?*
   — V. Hugo

4. *One has to multiply thoughts to the point where there aren't enough policemen to control them.*
   — S. J. Lee

5. *Just as wheat is not without straw, so no dream is without some nonsense.*
   — Talmud

6. *God is a geometrician.*
   — Plato

7. *It is always good when a man has two irons in the fire.*
   — F. Beaumont

8. *Part of the secret to success in life is to eat what you want and let the food fight it out inside.*
   — M. Twain

9. *Work without hope draws nectar in a sieve, and hope without an object cannot live.*
   — Coleridge

10. *Not only strike while the iron is hot, but make it hot by striking.*
    — O. Cromwell

11. *If you keep a thing seven years, you are sure to find a use for it.*
    — S. W. Scott

12. *It may be that you are not yourself luminous, but you are a conductor of light.*
    — A. Conan Doyle

13. *Thinking to get at once all the gold the goose could give, he killed it and opened it to find — nothing.*
    — Aesop

14. *Every French soldier carries a marshall's baton in his knapsack.*
    — N. Bonaparte

15. *If I have seen further, it is by standing on the shoulders of giants.*
    — I. Newton

Thinking
Style Inventory

Rank order the responses which describe your preferences to the following statements from 4 to 1. Number 4 represents your top preference. Number 1 represents your least preferred response to each situation.

1. When it comes to planning, I would prefer:

   ___ A. Coming up with a 10-year vision statement describing the direction our organization will take.

   ___ B. Researching and analyzing the facts and figures on which we might make projections.

   ___ C. Facilitating a planning session for our team.

   ___ D. Developing the plan after the research and the vision statement are completed.

2. Regarding my accountability for the financial aspect of my job, I prefer:

   ___ A. Providing and/or explaining financial reports.

   ___ B. Analyzing financial reports and making comparisons to other months, quarters, or years.

   ___ C. Utilizing financial reports only when necessary to support my interpretation of the big picture.

   ___ D. Informally talking with others who are qualified and willing to keep me informed.

3. Administrative duties I prefer are:

   ___ A. Dealing with human relations.

   ___ B. Insuring that established plans and procedures are followed.

   ___ C. Finding new ways to get the work done.

   ___ D. Working with numbers and data.

4. When it comes to problem solving, I prefer:

   ___ A. Researching the facts and/or figures in order to define the problem.

   ___ B. Discussing the problem with others in order to get different feelings and opinions about the situation.

   ___ C. Coming up with an innovative solution to the problem.

   ___ D. Implementing the agreed upon solution.

5. The training and development function I prefer is:

   ___ A. Working with people to tell them and show them how to do the job.

   ___ B. Analyzing and evaluating a person's performance and suggesting areas for improvement.

   ___ C. Challenging people to discover on their own and learn from their own experience.

   ___ D. Being sensitive to people's needs and assisting them in meeting those needs.

6. I tend to make decisions based on:
   ___ A. Logical step-by-step thinking.
   ___ B. Past experience.
   ___ C. My emotional reaction.
   ___ D. My insight and intuition.

7. When I wish to influence another person toward accepting my idea, I:
   ___ A. Develop a logical rationale that the person can't refute.
   ___ B. Walk the person through the details and sound principles of my idea, one step at a time.
   ___ C. Share reasons why my idea will bring personal satisfaction to that person.
   ___ D. Point out the unique factors of my idea which can open new vistas.

8. When choosing a new desk and chair for my office, I would:
   ___ A. Select a traditional style from a reputable firm.
   ___ B. Select from the store who gives me the best value and price.
   ___ C. Select the desk and chair which best fits the overall theme I've chosen for my office.
   ___ D. Select the desk and chair which feels good.

9. I prefer participating in meetings which include:
   ___ A. Brainstorming ideas.
   ___ B. Information exchange.
   ___ C. Team development.
   ___ D. Decision making.

10. I most value information which:
    ___ A. Separates facts from opinions, providing a base for analysis.
    ___ B. Provides personal meaning and stimulates motivation.
    ___ C. Can be put to use in producing results.
    ___ D. Offers hidden possibilities or new opportunities.

11. I enjoy participating in conversations with people when we can:
    ___ A. Express our honest feelings.
    ___ B. Have a healthy debate.
    ___ C. Come up with new ideas or insights.
    ___ D. Accomplish something.

12. When organizing, I prefer the task of:
    ___ A. Setting priorities and assigning work to the most capable person.
    ___ B. Considering the big picture and how everything will fit.
    ___ C. Controlling the steps, seeing to details.
    ___ D. Finding ways to ensure effective communication.

13. I have trouble communicating with people who:
    ___ A. Can't see the main point of what I'm trying to say.
    ___ B. Are insensitive to feelings.
    ___ C. Don't sequence their thoughts and constantly change the subject.
    ___ D. Who are illogical.

14. Rules that don't make sense should be:
    ___ A. Evaluated.
    ___ B. Followed.
    ___ C. Flexible.
    ___ D. Challenged.

15. My favorite leisure activities provide an opportunity for:
    ___ A. Emotional excitement.
    ___ B. Artistic expression.
    ___ C. Developing skills.
    ___ D. Exercising my mind.

16. I prefer my surroundings to be:
    ___ A. Mentally stimulating.
    ___ B. Neat and orderly.
    ___ C. Warm and friendly.
    ___ D. Appropriate.

17. When dining in a restaurant, I prefer one which:
    ___ A. Has ambience in accord with its gourmet food.
    ___ B. Is traditional, efficient, and I can count on for good service.
    ___ C. Provides intimacy, soft music, flowers and candlelight.
    ___ D. Is incomparable, in my opinion.

18. Work situations which excite me are:
    ___ A. Discovering a unique breakthrough solution for a chronic business problem.
    ___ B. Quantifying and therefore understanding how to make a difficult choice.
    ___ C. Completing an important project, one step at a time.
    ___ D. Negotiating a solution within a work group which is acceptable to all members.

19. What I like about vacations is:
    ___ A. Planning an itinerary and then experiencing my plan.
    ___ B. Having the freedom to do whatever I want on the spur of the moment.
    ___ C. Having time to be close with family and/or friends.
    ___ D. Having the opportunity to critique new places, cities, restaurants, and/or resorts.

20. Having read a book, I remember:
    ___ A. What I liked and/or didn't like.
    ___ B. The sequence of the story or content.
    ___ C. The emotions I experienced.
    ___ D. What I thought the author was trying to convey.

21. Those who really know my attributes would describe me as:
    ___ A. A visionary who sees the "big picture."
    ___ B. A logical decision maker.
    ___ C. An effective planner who follows through.
    ___ D. A responsive listener.

22. I have the most in common with people who:
    ___ A. Are supportive and sensitive to others' feelings.
    ___ B. Are willing to critique others' views.
    ___ C. Provide appropriate common sense answers when asked.
    ___ D. Are imaginative.

23. If included in developing a marketing strategy, I would most enjoy:
    ___ A. Analyzing all aspects of our competition in order to recommend the best positioning of our product and/or service.
    ___ B. Identifying the needs of consumers through empathy and intuition.
    ___ C. Predicting future trends in order to determine opportunities for innovation.
    ___ D. Reviewing past experiences, selecting strategies which have stood the test of time.

24. In developing my own five year wish list, it would include:
    ___ A. Planning for and controlling a work group who is charged with keeping my organization moving steadily forward.
    ___ B. Being the technical expert and consultant that the company looks to in times of crisis.
    ___ C. Being a mentor who helps people improve the quality of their lives.
    ___ D. Taking new risks which will give me an opportunity to grow.

Scoring Directions

Place your rankings for each question on the following score sheet, then total each column. The column with the highest score indicates your most preferred thinking style, and the column with the lowest indicates your least preferred style.

THINKING STYLE INVENTORY SCORE SHEET

	ANALYZER	IMPLEMENTOR	COLLABORATOR	IMAGINATOR
1.	___ B.	___ D.	___ C.	___ A.
2.	___ B.	___ A.	___ D.	___ C.
3.	___ D.	___ B.	___ A.	___ C.
4.	___ A.	___ D.	___ B.	___ C.
5.	___ B.	___ A.	___ D.	___ C.
6.	___ A.	___ B.	___ C.	___ D.
7.	___ A.	___ B.	___ C.	___ D.
8.	___ B.	___ A.	___ D.	___ C.
9.	___ D.	___ B.	___ C.	___ A.
10.	___ A.	___ C.	___ B.	___ D.
11.	___ B.	___ D.	___ A.	___ C.
12.	___ A.	___ C.	___ D.	___ B.
13.	___ D.	___ C.	___ B.	___ A.
14.	___ A.	___ B.	___ C.	___ D.
15.	___ D.	___ C.	___ A.	___ B.
16.	___ D.	___ B.	___ C.	___ A.
17.	___ D.	___ B.	___ C.	___ A.
18.	___ B.	___ C.	___ D.	___ A.
19.	___ D.	___ A.	___ C.	___ B.
20.	___ A.	___ B.	___ C.	___ D.
21.	___ B.	___ C.	___ D.	___ A.
22.	___ B.	___ C.	___ A.	___ D.
23.	___ A.	___ D.	___ B.	___ C.
24.	___ B.	___ A.	___ C.	___ D.
Totals	_____	_____	_____	_____

Parallel Worlds

PARALLEL WORLDS

American Literature	Geography	Perversions
Animal Kingdom	Geology	Philosophy
Animal Husbandry	Gourmet Food	Photography
Architecture	Great Documents	Physics
Art	Great Religious Books	Politics
Astrology	Ibsen	Pornography
Astronomy	Insects	Psychology
Biology	Inventions	Revolutionary War
Bowling	Journalism	Shakespeare
Comics	Jungle	Soap Operas
Composers	Law	Social Movements
Computers	Machines	Space
Dance	Manufacturing	Stamps and Coins
Economics	Medicine	Television Sitcoms
Education	Medicine	Tennis
Electronics	Meteorology	Theatre
Entertainment	Monuments	Transplants
Evolution	Movies	Transportation
Finance	Mysteries	Vietnam
Fishing	Mythology	Wild West
Flying	Nutrition	Wine
Football	Oriental Food	WW II

PCP Expanded

MENTAL EVENTS SLIDE SHOW (Events 4-8)

PCP EXAMPLE

(Key Column) Implementation Events	(Insight Column)
4. Both research and plant people involved are notified of the changes to take place in a joint two-day problem solving meeting held off-site at a business conf. center. This meeting is chaired jointly by the VP of R&D and the VP of Mfg. 5. The VP of Marketing meets with the vice presidents of plant manufacturing and R&D to discuss the need for a cross discipline team of R&D and plant people at the plant working on facing manufacturing system. 6. The Director of New Product Marketing meets with the VP of Marketing (the most powerful person in the company aside from the CEO) to talk about the need for an ad hoc team of R&D/Plant people to solve the problem. 7. The Marketing Mgr. of diaper facing meets with the director of new product marketing to present the R&D solution to the diaper facing problem and to suggest that the VP of Marketing is the only person powerful enough to bring this joint team from R&D and the plant into existence. 8. The Research Mgr. of diaper facing meets with the Research Asst. Dir. of New Product Development, Marketing Mgr. of diaper facing, and Asst. Plant Mgr. for diaper facing to present his proposal.	

ACTIVITIES LIST

PCP EXAMPLE

(Key Column) Implementation Events	(Insight Column) Activities for Next Step
10. (Present - 3/1) The creative session has ended. The research manager's solution is to create an ad hoc team of research scientists and plant engineers which will be lead by a joint, two-person team consisting of the Asst. Director of New Product Dev. and the Asst. Plant Manager for diaper facing. The operation's responsibility will fall to the Research Manager who will have both the R&D scientists and a portion of the plant engineers reporting directly to him. He, in turn, reports periodically in problem solving meetings to the two-person committee.	

PCP EXAMPLE (CONTINUED)

(Key Column) Implementation Events	(Insight Column) Activities for Next Step
The operation is located in the QC portion of the plant. Meanwhile a small group of plant engineers will be temporarily transferred to the R&D facility to report to the Director of New Product Dev. They are to learn about emerging technologies and fill the void created by the scientists who left for the plant. The whole issue must be resolved, and the plant operations must show significant improvement in six months.	
9. (3/8) The Research Mgr. of diaper facing meets with his boss, the Asst. Director of New Product Development, to present the R&D solution and ask for help in the implementation.	A. A marketing strategy document stating the solution, the necessary human and technical resources to make it work, and a rationale showing the proposal as the only reasonable hope of solving the problem in the six-month time frame. B. Convince him to relocate temporarily to the plant. (Completion time: 1 week)
8. (3/8) The Research Mgr. of diaper facing meets with the Research Asst. Dir. of New Product Development, Marketing Mgr. of diaper facing, and Asst. Plant Mgr. for diaper facing to present his proposal.	A. Availability of Asst. Plant Mgr., Asst. Dir. of NPD, and Mktg. Mgr. all in the same place at the same time. B. Buy-in from Asst. Plant Mgr. (Completion time: 1 week)
7. (3/17) The Marketing Mgr. of diaper facing meets with the Director of New Product Marketing to present the R&D solution to the diaper facing problem and to suggest that the VP of Marketing is the only person powerful enough to bring this joint team from R&D and the plant into existance.	A. Availability of Director of New Product Marketing. (Completion time: 2 days)
6. (3/24) The Director of New Product Marketing meets with the VP of Marketing (the most powerful person in the company aside from the CEO) to talk about the need for an ad hoc team of R&D/Plant people to solve the commercialization problem.	A. Availability of marketing funds to cover some relocation costs. B. Buy-in by VP of Marketing. C. A marketing strategy document consistent with the timing of the solution. (Completion time: 1 week)
5. (3/28) The VP of Marketing meets with the Vice Presidents of plant manufacturing and R&D to discuss the need for a cross discipline team of R&D and plant people to be headquartered at the plant working on the diaper facing manufacturing system.	A. Crucial acceptance by VPs of both plant mfg. and R&D to commit to the notion of power sharing. B. A slippage of 3-6 months in new product development while Asst. Dir. of Pdt. Extension takes over for Asst. Dir. of NPD at R&D. (Completion time: 1 week)

PCP EXAMPLE (CONTINUED)

(Key Column) Implementation Events	(Insight Column) Activities for Next Step
4. (4/21) Both research and plant people involved are notified of the changes to take place in a joint two-day problem solving meeting held off-site at a business conf. center. This meeting is chaired jointly by the VP of R&D and the VP of Manufacturing.	A. Developing format for interdisciplinary meeting. B. Finding appropriate meeting site and conference facilities on short notice. C. Developing shared understanding and commitment of all people involved in change. D. Working out all ancillary problems involved in transition. (Completion time: 3 weeks)
3. (5/12) The Asst. Dir. of NPD and a portion of the R&D Dept. has just temporarily relocated to the plant, and have taken over a portion of the plant QC lab. Concurrently, some of the plant engineers have temporarily transferred to R&D where they are reporting directly to the Director of New Product Development.	A. Relocation and moving schedules approved. B. QC lab modified. C. Arrangements with local plant-area motel owners secured. D. Specialized equipment shipped and set up. E. Plant people transferred to R&D site and living in motels at R&D headquarters. (Completion time: 3 weeks)
2. (5/19) A team building session has been held with all the players at the plant to develop a new vision and to discuss roles and responsibilities. The meeting is chaired by the Asst. Director of New Product Development and by the Asst. Plant Manager.	A. Format worked out for joint task team meeting. B. Facilitators appointed and schooled in shared creative problem solving techniques. C. Developing new esprit in joint team. D. New roles and responsibilities agreed to by all participants. (Completion time: 3½ months)
1. (9/1) R&D and plant people are working together at the plant instituting quick fixes as well as developing a long term understanding of the commercialization process. They are led by a mgmt. team of the Asst. Research Director and the Asst. Plant Manager.	A. Commercial process analyzed for short-term fixes. B. Long-term understanding work completed. C. All workers working with facing participating in quality and productivity problem-solving sessions. D. Commercial quantities of on-spec goods produced for the market. (Completion time: 3½ months)

ACTIVITIES REVIEW

SLIDE SHOW EVENT	#9. Marketing meeting with the Asst. Director of New Product Marketing.

	ACTIVITY	RATING	RATIONALE
1.	Marketing strategy document.	3	It is easy to show how the R&D solution is the only thing compatible with marketing strategy.
2.	Convincing him to relocate temporarily to the plant.	1	It will be difficult to get him to agree to relocate.

SLIDE SHOW EVENT	#8. Marketing meeting with the VP of Marketing.

ACTIVITY	RATING	RATIONALE
1. Availability of marketing funds to cover relocation costs.	2	Within budget limits. Show how solution is cost effective.
2. Buy-in by VP of Marketing.	2	Feather in his cap to show how he can catalyze the interdisciplinary team. Shows his ability to take over for the CEO when he retires.

SLIDE SHOW EVENT	#7. Meeting with Marketing Mgr., Asst. R&D Director, and Asst. Plant Manager.

ACTIVITY	RATING	RATIONALE
1. Availability of all people in meeting.	3	All people available for monthly meeting anyway.
2. Buy-in from Asst. Plant Manager.	3	Willingness to get R&D help to make the venture a commercial success.

SLIDE SHOW EVENT	#6. Marketing meeting with Director of New Product Marketing.

ACTIVITY	RATING	RATIONALE
1. Marketing Strategy document.	3	Easy to show how R&D solution is the only thing compatible with the marketing strategy.

SLIDE SHOW EVENT	#5 VP meeting with Marketing, Manufacturing, and R&D.

ACTIVITY	RATING	RATIONALE
1. Acceptance of VPs of Manufacturing and R&D to power sharing.	2	VP of Marketing has ear of CEO, a chance for Mfg. and R&D to show they are team players to the CEO.
2. Slippage of 3-6 months in NPD while Asst. Director of Line Extension takes over for Asst. Director of NPD at R&D.	✓1	Slippage puts PCP behind competitors in New Technology Development.

SLIDE SHOW EVENT	#4 Two-day problem solving meeting about task force.

ACTIVITY	RATING	RATIONALE
1. Developing format for interdisciplinary meeting.	3	Easy planning task and VP Mfg. and R&D are good planners.
2. Finding appropriate meeting site and conference facilities on short notice.	2	It's off-season for resorts and there are probably many accommodations available. We will use head of traffic dept. to find appropriate place.

ACTIVITY	RATING	RATIONALE
3. Developing shared understanding and commitment of all.	✓1	Some of the plant and R&D people will be resistant, especially those who have to relocate.
4. Working out all ancillary problems.	2	Special training for facilitators prior to group problem solving session. We will also use the consultants who helped us develop the solution.

SLIDE SHOW EVENT	#3 The Move.

ACTIVITY	RATING	RATIONALE
1. Relocation and moving schedules approved.	3	Traffic and Human Resources join forces to facilitate schedules and procedures.
2. Quality control labs modified to accommodate new research staff.	2	QC labs will defer testing for diaper facing to R&D/Mfg. team. Also will use part of warehouse to accommodate new space requirement.
3. Arrangements with plant-area motel owners.	3	The motel owners stand to make a lot of money.
4. Specialized equipment shipped and set up.	2	Business moving company contracted. Their liaison works with Traffic, HRD, and Mgr. of Diaper Facing — R&D.
5. Plant people transferred to R&D site and set up in motels around R&D facility.	2	An opportunity to get acquainted with latest technology and to experience cultural opportunities of big city close to R&D location. Also handled by Traffic, plant HRD, and psychological consultant to help in adapting to change.

SLIDE SHOW EVENT	#2 Team building session with the Ad Hoc Team.

ACTIVITY	RATING	RATIONALE
1. Format worked out for meeting.	3	Easy planning task.
2. Facilitator appointed and schooled in shared creative problem solving techniques.	3	Facilitators have already had experience from Event D. They will also receive additional training from CPS consultants.
3. Developing new esprit in team. New roles and responsibilities agreed to by everyone.	2	Develop a creative environment where everyone participates in development of new team vision. Everyone Is rewarded when outcome is successful. Everyone gets to go to Hawaii for one week at the end of the assignment with their families at no cost, and as compensatory time, so it doesn't cut into vacations.

	SLIDE SHOW EVENT		#1 Future State.

	ACTIVITY	RATING	RATIONALE
1.	Commercial process analyzed for short-term fixes.	2	Change in SOPs where machine is stopped when producing well, *and* producing poorly, to compare operational differences.
2.	Long-term fundamental understanding work completed.	1	Might not have the necessary expertise to support practical application with theoretical work.
3.	All workers participate in creative problem solving quality and productivity sessions.	3	This has been set up by two previous meetings, especially Event B.
4.	Commercial quantities of "on-spec" items produced for market.	1-2	If we can change all other ones into twos, we have a better than 50/50 chance of successful completion within required time.

PROBLEM ACTIVITIES

SLIDE SHOW EVENT	#8 Meeting between the Research Manager and the Assistant Director of New Product Development.

ACTIVITY

Proposal and rationale acceptance by the Assistant Director of R&D and Director of New Product Development.

OBSTACLE

It will be difficult to get the Assistant Director of New Product Development to agree to relocate.

HOW TOs. . .

How to get buy-in from the Assistant Director of New Product Development

How to get him to see the personal benefit

How to coerce him into accepting the job

How to flatter him into accepting the job

✓ How to show him how this might help him get ahead in his career

IDEAS

Show him how he will be largely responsible for success.

Show him how new task will broaden his skills.

Show him how the VP of R&D will leverage this project into a promotion for him.

✓ Get the Marketing Manager for diaper facing to talk with him.

✓ Show him that he is the only one who can pull it off.

WHAT'S USEFUL about having the marketing manager talk to him and show him that he's the only one who can do the job?

The marketing manager has his ear.

It creates a power position for the marketing manager and makes him a high profile person.

He will be recognized by the VP of Marketing.

WHAT'S MISSING?

How to get the marketing manager to talk with him

IDEAS

Simply ask. There shouldn't be any obstacle.

SLIDE SHOW EVENT	#4 Meeting with VP of Marketing, VP of Manufacturing, and VP of R&D.

ACTIVITY

Slippage of 3-6 months in new product development while the Assistant Director of Line Extension takes over for the Assistant Director of NPD at R&D.

OBSTACLE

The slippage puts PCP behind competitors in new technology development.

HOW TOs. . .

How to keep up with competition

✓ How to avoid slippage

How to bring Line Extension Director up to speed

How to manage new technology from a remote location

IDEAS

Institute technology transfer sessions between Assistant Director of NPD and the Line Extension Director.

Have remote teleconferencing sessions between the two every Friday afternoon.

Set up teleconferencing meetings with all R&D professionals at the plant and their technical counterparts from R&D for mutual information exchange and direction.

✓ Use commercialization learning at plant site to refocus R&D new technology work to create short implementation schedule. Lost time for new product thrust in R&D gets repaid in subsequent commercialization attempts. Use the above mentioned teleconferencing meetings to exchange this information between the plant and R&D.

IDEA ACCEPTED

Because the opportunity to shorten commercialization for all future projects is so exciting, it more than offsets the time-lag problem, and brings the rating of 1 to a 3.

SLIDE SHOW EVENT	#3 Two-day problem solving meeting with an inter-group task force.

ACTIVITY

Developing shared understanding and commitment of all people involved in the change.

OBSTACLE

Some of the plant and R&D people will resist because the move will upset their family and personal lives.

HOW TOs. . .

How to make everyone happy

How to get commitment from those who are reluctant

How to minimize the impact on their home and personal lives

✓ How to involve families in the change

IDEAS

Have a dinner meeting with everyone involved and their families. Have the CEO give a talk about the importance of the project to the success of the company. Involve liberal travel allowance for families on weekends. Set up a transition service in the corporation for the families involved to help them with problems arising in the relocation.

WHAT'S USEFUL?

It involves the families of the employees of the corporation.

It shows employees that the corporation is highly aware of their special and unique contribution.

It shows appreciation and concern for individuals.

WHAT'S MISSING?

How to get the CEO to give the talk

IDEAS

Get the VP of Marketing to convince him to do it.

If he isn't available, have him make a videotape to be presented at the dinner, with the VP of Human Resources to handle specific questions and concerns.

IDEAS ACCEPTED

The combination of these two ideas leaves nothing missing. Chances are good that the CEO will want to make the speech, and that it will significantly help change the attitudes of those reluctant to make the move.

SLIDE SHOW EVENT   #1 Future State

ACTIVITY

Fundamental long-term understanding work is completed.

OBSTACLE

We may not have the necessary in-house expertise for the theoretical work.

HOW TOs. . .

How to complete fundamental understanding work

How to get the theoretical expertise

✓ How to buy theoretical expertise

How to lure theoretical expertise

How to develop theoretical expertise

IDEAS for buying theoretical expertise.

Contract with a local university.

Contract with a high-technology consulting firm such as A.D. Little, the Battelle Institute, etc.

✓ Contract with an academic who has written widely about new technology.

Contract with equipment manufacturer for their theoretical person, depending upon the results of analysis that shows which piece of equipment is causing the most problems.

WHAT'S USEFUL?

We already have someone with whom we have worked.

He doesn't mind long-term commitment as he is on sabbatical and needs the money.

We might be able to hire him as a permanent employee.

WHAT'S MISSING?

Nothing.

SELLING THE IDEA

A. VP of Marketing

He always talks about "the big picture." He dresses flamboyantly, and his office has several pieces of art work in it. He gets bored very easily in meetings once he understands the agenda's major thrust. He endlessly doodles crazy geometric designs on a scratch pad. He is definitely an Imaginator. Present ideas to him by showing the overall concept with an attached flow diagram briefly outlining the significant events. Then point out why this solution is different from anything PCP has ever attempted in the past.

B. Asst. Director of New Product Development

He searches for facts and figures. Driven by "quantity," he always seeks to compare results and hypotheses to other published results. He prides himself on being a "gatekeeper" and his ability to ask probing questions about the efficacy of any approach. He is an Analyzer. Approach him armed with huge amounts of data about machine performance comparing situations where R&D is present and absent from the mill. Show him that he is the only one "smart enough" to be able to oversee the technical approaches that are being pursued.

C. Marketing Manager — Diaper Facing

His desk is forever buried beneath paper. He works on five projects at once, but unlike the VP of Marketing, he is very involved in people-oriented projects like the United Way. He is both an Imaginator and a Collaborator. Show him the overall concept too, but emphasize how it will change the ways in which people work together.

D. Director of New Product Marketing

Although he models himself after the Vice President of Marketing, he always finds himself involved in detail. He takes forever to make decisions; he is always requesting more data. But once he gets the data, he gets tangled up in his underwear when trying to decipher it. Although he sees himself as an Imaginator, he is really an Implementor. Spend one or two minutes on the big picture, but pay particular attention to the details of each step referring to the improved facing attributes resulting from the plan and how they impact the consumer.

231

E. Plant Manager — Diaper System

"Standard Operating Procedure" is this guy's middle name. He has an immaculately clean office, and he forever worries more about how neat the manufacturing floor is rather than the quality of the product he is producing. He is definitely an Implementor. Present a series of new SOPs to rid the clutter and ambiguity clouding the ways business is currently being done.

F. Assistant Plant Manager — Diaper Facing

His main concern is the comfort level of the people working on the machines. He coaches a local soccer team in his spare time and is always in personnel worrying about how new policies and procedures will affect his people. He spends a lot of time on the manufacturing floor talking with machine operators about their personal problems. He is a Collaborator. Emphasize the notion of Creative Problem Solving *teams*; Collaborators value teamwork. Explain that these teams ask workers to contribute their ideas to solve plant problems and that the teams would offer him and his people new opportunities for personal and professional growth.

G. VP of R&D and VP of Manufacturing

They are an Implementor and Analyzer, respectively. However, they will rubber stamp any decision that the VP of Marketing feels strongly about. Let the VP of Marketing sell them.

DEVELOPING RISK INSURANCE
A. Analysis Of Lost Time May Prove Too Difficult

This is a problem because if we can't figure out what's causing the breakdown on the machines, we won't be able to develop any short-term fix. If this happens, we either shut the operation down and transfer everyone back to work in the lab, or do something else. The first option is not acceptable. We need to think about "something else." We might need to reinforce ourselves with consultants who can help us with the data analysis.

We have one consultant in the Technical Information Department at R&D. The VP of R&D will ask the Director of Technical Information to lend us this person for at least five months. Nobody every pays attention to those guys anyway; it will give him a chance to shine.

We also need an expert in design experiments who can help us minimize the variables. There is a person who teaches a course in this at the local college. I think he would love to help us. We also need a computer expert to help us measure the machine condition data more frequently making it easier for us to spot trends and see cause-effect relationships between machine conditions and performance. All of these consultants are available to us, which reduces this problem to a lower probability of occurrence.

B. Long-term Fix Might Require Major Rebuild Of The Machine

If this is true, then the machine in its present configuration doesn't stand a ghost of a chance of ever producing high quality product consistently. We would then go back to the lab and dedicate three-quarters of our R&D people to the simultaneous development of the next generation of products and to building a machine capable of manufacturing them.

While taking this major step, we would leave a skeleton R&D crew at the plant on rotation, so we would have perhaps one-quarter of the committed resources at the plant at any one time. The R&D people would each spend one week a month at the plant. This creates a tenuous holding pattern with the current inferior product for about 15 months, but it allows us to be clearly the number one product in the future by learning from our commercialization mistakes while we develop great new products.

C. Technical Consultant Might Not Be Available

This is a problem because we won't have the theoretical depth to do the type of fundamental understanding work necessary for long-term improvement. We could minimize this problem by enlisting the help of the Director of Basic Research. She has a young scientist who has studied with the consultant, and even though she's working on important long-term projects of her own, this would certainly take precedence. Also we could ask the consultant to suggest other people in the same field who he feels are smart enough and have studied these types of phenomena sufficiently to make a good theoretical consultant. With these two options we minimize this problem.

However, I think we need to have the mechanical engineering department develop and construct a working scale model of the machinery that we can run at high speed back at R&D. This would probably cost us one-third man year in salary and an additional $10,000 in expenses, but it would be well worth the effort and expenditure. We actually would have the theoretical consultant overseeing the design and construction of the model. We would then minimize the additional human resources needed.

D. New Technology Introduction By Competitor

There's no question that we lose some valuable time in R&D with this move. However, the valuable learning that takes place for our research people in a commercial environment, in terms of both technical and interpersonal skill-building, makes our R&D response take longer than it would if we didn't commit resources this way. But it also greatly shortens the commercialization period of any response with the new technology we make.

Actually, it seems that we lose very little if our competitor develops a new innovation in this six month period. We don't have to concern ourselves with this. It might even be a positive situation.

E. The Union May Prove To Be A Difficult Obstacle

Certainly if the union is not supportive of what we're trying to do, they can screw it all up. We need to get them on our side so we're all pulling together. I think one of the things we might do is offer training in team problem solving as a free course to any union member who chooses to attend and perhaps pay them overtime for attending. The problem with the facing has generated plenty of lucrative overtime for union members so they are actually rewarded when the machine fails. We may want to offset lost overtime with challenging production goals with bonuses for reaching them.

We also need to show the union that we're treating their members not just as a pair of hands, but as people with intelligent, imaginative, fertile minds who's ideas are valued as much as their physical labor. We need to have a meeting with the shop stewards to introduce these new ways of working together and encourage their participation in solving any problems that may result as a consequence of this new system. I think we can get their cooperation and turn this potential negative into a positive benefit for the plant.

ATTITUDE CHECK

"It appears that the whole success of this undertaking lies in the ability to consolidate the leadership of important parts of manufacturing and R&D under one flag. With a CEO too far removed from the day-to-day business to be of any help here, the only other one who has the clout and the power to make this happen is the Vice President of Marketing. It appears that his leadership and support is more important than any of the other criteria I've developed. In my bicycle analogy, he is my parents, and asking for his financial and attitudinal support is like asking for a bicycle for my paper route. I've rated his acceptance of this proposal as a two because I can think of no logical reason for him not to support this endeavour. However, I could think of no logical reason for my parents not to get me my bicycle. I guess I'm worried that if this doesn't work, if I can't carry this off, I'll be on his black list forever, and it will ruin my PCP career.

"On the other hand, I can't think of any reason why he won't be supportive. It seems to me that I have two issues emerging here. One is How to guarantee his support of the project, or how to make my rating of two, a three.

"And having done this, How to minimize the downside risk to my career if, by some circumstance, we do the project and it fails. I think I need to tackle the last problem first, because if I can solve that, I'll have additional energy for developing a full-blown campaign that will make the marketing VP's buy-in a certainty.

"How to minimize downside risk to my career."

> A check mark beside an idea indicates it has been chosen for the next stage of development.

IDEAS

Find out in advance what might happen.

Prepare my resume just in case.

✓ Involve the VP in the creative problem solving necessary to make our solution work.

WHAT'S USEFUL? (About involving the VP.)

If he's part of the problem solving, we're in the same boat, and his power will help keep the boat floating.

He may have points of view that will be useful to me in dealing with the manufacturing organization.

He will become more involved in future R&D projects, helping us to focus better.

WHAT'S MISSING?

How to involve the VP in the problem solving for the solution.

IDEAS

✓ Approach him directly in an informal setting.

✓ Ask for his critique of the plan I've already developed.

✓ Ask for his help in getting the attitudinal acceptance that I need from potentially reluctant participants both from the plant and from R&D.

✓ Show him all the potential marketing spin-offs from this new way of working.

WHAT'S USEFUL?

All these ideas are right on and will help me involve him.

WHAT'S MISSING?

How to approach him informally.

IDEAS

Find out as much as I can about not only his styles and preferences, but about his values, hobbies, the way he structures his leisure time, his work habits. Determine if we both have someone in common that will be an advocate for me, someone the VP respects and admires.

WHAT'S MISSING?

How to find the right person

IDEAS

Ask the marketing manager.

Ask the marketing director.

✓ Ask the VP's secretary. She might be the appropriate person.

WHAT'S USEFUL?

The VP's secretary is respected.

She knows the VP very well.

Everyone knows that she has a lot of influence with him.

WHAT'S MISSING?

How to approach the VP's secretary

IDEAS

Ask my secretary, with whom I have a positive business relationship. She is best friends with the VP's secretary.

WHAT'S MISSING?

Nothing!

THE FINAL STEP

FIRST STEP

The very first step is to meet with my secretary.

PEOPLE INVOLVED

Me (the R&D Manager)

Andrea (my secretary)

THINKING STYLE

She's very "people-oriented" and she loves team work. She's probably a Collaborator.

BEST TIME

Lunch would be the best time to talk to her.

LOCATION

She loves the food and atmosphere at Andretti's.

DECLARATION

I will take my secretary to lunch either tomorrow or the next day, depending on her availability.

Index

BUSINESS AND PROFESSIONAL BOOKS

MegaTraits $17.95
Dr. Doris Lee McCoy 1-55622-056-1

Dr. McCoy traveled extensively to interview over 1,000 "successful" people. Interviews with such people as Charlton Heston, Malcolm Forbes, and Ronald Reagan led Dr. McCoy to discover 12 traits of success. She sought consistencies and success patterns from which you can benefit. Are there specific points to help all of us become more successful? The answer is a resounding YES! There are traits consistently found in the lives of successful people. Read *MegaTraits* to discover how you too can develop and utilize these unique attributes.

Business Emotions $14.95
Richard Contino 1-55622-058-8

Revolutionize your thinking, conditioning, and approach. Learn why emotions are a controlling factor in every success and failure situation. This practical book will guide you through the maze of hidden psychological issues in a simple and straightforward manner. Achieve predictable, positive, and immediate results.

Innovation, Inc. $12.95
Stephen Grossman, Bruce Rodgers, 1-55622-054-5
Beverly Moore

Unlock your hidden potential to reach a new plane of creative thinking. Seek out new avenues of problem-solving by elevating your ability to conceive ideas. Techniques and exercises in this book expand your creativity. The authors take you on a journey designed to spark confidence by reorganizing your thinking processes and patterns. Learn to use innovative thinking to inspire fresh ideas and formulate imaginative concepts.

Investor Beware $14.95
Henry Rothenberg 1-55622-055-3

Create your own luck with this book detailing the essentials for safe investments. Avoid shady, risky, and unsuccessful investments. Learn how to anticipate and interpret various investment climates and analyze a business from financial statements. The average investor will find what he needs to know about economics, financing, taxes, operating entities, and types of investments. Discover the ramifications of diversified investments such as real estate, franchises, oil and gas, gold, tax shelters, and syndications.

Steps to Strategic Management $13.95
Rick Molz 1-55622-050-2

This book is the story of one individual. . .YOU. Put yourself in the shoes of Joe Clancy, the imaginary entrepreneur in this book. By following the clear, ongoing example of Joe, you will discover how strategic management works. A series of nine steps will help you develop a systematic approach to strategic management. With honesty and hard work, you can use this book to help shape your future.

Call Wordware Publishing, Inc. for names of the bookstores in your area.
(214) 423-0090